Premium Essay on Peace.

THE RIGHT WAY;

OR,

THE GOSPEL APPLIED

TO

THE INTERCOURSE OF INDIVIDUALS AND NATIONS.

BY REV. JOSEPH A. COLLIER,

PASTOR OF THE REFORMED DUTCH CHURCH, GENEVA, N. Y.

PUBLISHED BY THE

AMERICAN TRACT SOCIETY,

150 NASSAU-STREET, NEW YORK.

A premium of $500, offered by the late Rev. THOMAS A. MERRILL, D. D., of Middlebury, Vt., was awarded to the author of this work by Rev. Joseph W. Parker, D. D., Rev. Asa D. Smith, D. D., and Hon. William J. Hubbard, judges. Dr. Merrill also appropriated the further sum of $600, for publishing and perpetuating the volume in the "Evangelical Family Library" of the American Tract Society.

CONTENTS.

PART I.

THE GOSPEL APPLIED TO THE INTERCOURSE OF INDIVIDUALS.

PART II.

THE GOSPEL APPLIED TO THE INTERCOURSE OF NATIONS.

CHAPTER XII

CHAPTER XIII.

CHAPTER XIV.

CHAPTER XV.

CHAPTER XVI.

THE RIGHT WAY.

PART I.

THE GOSPEL APPLIED TO THE INTERCOURSE OF INDIVIDUALS.

CHAPTER I.

INTRODUCTORY.

SUPPOSE we were gifted with the power of beholding at a glance the whole family of man, and of penetrating into all those mysterious relations and connections which exist between its different members, what a wonderful spectacle would present itself. We should see about a thousand millions of human beings, all more or less associated with and dependent upon one another, each contributing his share to the common happiness or misery, and each in turn receiving a certain proportion of both from others. We should see them all connected by those various ties of kindred, friendship, business, neighborhood, and country, which, perpetually interlacing one another, are spread like network over the whole earth. Beginning with the first and most sacred of all social institutions, the family, we should discover radiating from it circle after circle of human companionship, each extending wider than the last, until all are bounded by that one which engirdles the globe itself, the great brotherhood of man.

If we here suspended our gaze, and paused to reflect upon this wonderful arrangement of divine Providence, our thoughts might be such as these. What an admirable display of infinite wisdom! What a merciful provision of our good Creator for the welfare of his creatures! But are these beings adapted to the proper improvement and enjoyment of such a blessing? We see that in some respects they are. They are endowed with fine affections and tender sympathies, which are capable of conferring the most exquisite pleasure, and which their very relations to one another are fitted to cultivate and strengthen. If, then, they are governed by these better instincts of their nature; if they delight in the constant exercise of good will, and the constant interchange of kind actions, their companionship must perpetually foster their warm affections, and these in turn must add a charm to all their intercourse, and they cannot be otherwise than happy. If, on the other hand, they crush these kindly dispositions, and habitually cherish enmity or resentment instead of love, then these many-linked ties are converted from a blessing into a curse; for then they must be the means of nurturing foul passions, which grow by exercise, and greatly imbitter men's companionship. *The proportion in which the one or the other of these principles prevails, is the measure of the good or evil results of human intercourse.*

Confining our attention for the present to the sphere of ordinary social life, let us ask, What are the principles that commonly govern, and the good or evil results that commonly attend our intercourse *as individuals?*

We have only to contemplate the surface of society, to discover that many are actuated not by kindly and loving dispositions, but by those that are selfish and unloving; and that thus those very relations which are designed for our mutual good, are frequently turned into instruments of mutual wretchedness. We see many yielding without shame to the violence of angry passions. We see friendships blighted and consumed with their fierce heat, fond ties cruelly rent asunder, now a warm heart broken to appease them, and now a valued life cut down as their sacrifice. They array man against man, neighbor against neighbor, and brother against brother in wordy battle, and at times in fatal conflict. It is indeed frequently the case that the nearer the relation and the stronger the tie, the more hotly burn these flames in one or another of their forms, scathing both the bosom that cherishes them and those who may be their immediate objects.

This evil is almost as wide-spread as humanity itself. We often discover it in *the family*, destroying its peace, causing alienated hearts and estranged affections, and turning that inner sanctuary of human love into an abode of unhappy discord. We see it in *the school*, which in this respect, as in so many others, is a faithful picture of the active world. We see it in *the neighborhood*, casting its blight over the sweet influences of social life, and sowing broadcast the seeds of dissension. We see it in the more general intercourse of men, as they mingle in the busy mart and in scenes of daily enterprise and labor. We see it in *the church*, disgracing the cause of Christ and impeding pious effort, by arraying in opposition those who should know only a common sympathy. Wherever man is found, and under whatever circumstances or relations, his companionship is liable to be imbittered by strife.

Now *why* do we thus suffer? Why do so many hearts thus bleed and break, and so many lives become thus saddened? Must we regard this evil as a necessary element of our existence—a part of our endowment by the Creator? No; we cannot justly charge it upon God, nor upon any other than *ourselves*. We need not search far to discover its cause. The very existence of so dire a curse sufficiently indicates *some vast error*, of which this is the necessary fruit and penalty. If we look a little further, we shall behold that error in the practice of the *wrong way* of conducting intercourse and settling differences. This is the secret of the terrible woe in every one of its forms. It accounts for the wholesale slaughter of the battle-field, and for the petty quarrel that vexes its two or three angry disputants; for the blow which is murder in the sight of the law, and for much of that secret hate which is murder in the sight of God.

Differences must necessarily occur among men. As long as human nature is in its present state, we cannot expect to see a perfect harmony of views and feelings. We are so constituted that all cannot behold a subject in the same light, nor honestly coincide in the same opinions. But is it therefore necessary that there be strife and bloodshed? Must men persist in blinding themselves to reason, and to all the better feelings of their nature, because of these differences with one another?

Let us view it candidly and dispassionately. A man conceives himself injured by an angry word. Immediately the hot blood boils, fierce passions burn within him, the indignant retort quickly follows, and bitterest feelings are aroused upon both sides. If reason, conscience, or experience utter their voice, their appeals are lost in the clamors of the one overmastering passion which now like a tyrant possesses the whole souls and bodies of its victims. Each strives to surpass the other in the harshness of his invectives, until a wide breach is formed between them, and they perhaps try to decide their differences with blows. Now is this the *Right Way*, which thus answers passion with passion, wrong with wrong, and blow with blow; which, because the one party is beside himself, converts the other for the moment into a voluntary madman, and which permits the most endearing ties to be sundered by an inconsiderate word or casual error? Does it not rather prove itself by all its tendencies, by its bitter fruits, which have so filled the world with misery, and by its own very nature, to be emphatically the *wrong way?*

We would especially view it as a way that is *morally* wrong, or as constituting not only an evil to ourselves, but a sin against God. In proof of this we shall appeal to an authority that is far above all worldly custom, or the dictates of any merely human rule of duty—*the revealed will of God.* The precepts we shall present are the irrepealable edicts of the great Lawgiver of the universe; and we cannot evade them on account of their seeming difficulties, unpopularity, or distastefulness. The commands, "Thou shalt love thy neighbor as thyself," "Love your enemies," "Resist not evil," and the many others of similar import, have as strong a claim upon our obedience as the commands, "Thou shalt not kill," "Thou shalt not steal," etc. Indeed, they are in effect the same laws; for "whosoever hateth his brother is a murderer," 1 John 3:15, and "love is the fulfilling of the law." Rom. 13:10. If, then, there is any obligation in religion—if God's revealed will, and not our perverse inclination, is the rule of human duty, and if we are to be judged by that rule according to our deeds, with what solemn weight these precepts are invested! How authoritative their every word and syllable. How awful their binding power, how terrible their penalties. Let us bring to their consideration hearts humbly obedient and docile, and prepared to accept, as our plain guide to duty, the *whole* of the gospel of our Lord Jesus Christ.

The gospel of Christ is eminently practical. While addressing itself to *man as he is*, it also reveals to us *man as he ought to be*. Its precepts are exactly adapted to our nature and circumstances, and are capable of application to our ordinary, every-day life. As we now consider a few of those relating to human intercourse, we shall see that they present the only practicable method of relief from the evils that surround us. As one by one they unfold to our view in all their sublimity and loveliness, let us adore the wisdom that has framed, and the grace that has revealed them; and let us regard them in their true character, as not only beautiful in theory, but most divinely beautiful *in practice.*

The gospel views man as sustaining relations both to God and to his fellow-men. It clearly defines those relations, and points out the duties growing from them. It applies itself, first of all, to the regulation of our intercourse with God. To this end, it corrects the erroneous views of Him which are generally entertained, condemns the false and prescribes the true mode of worship, and while teaching the utter uselessness of every other way of seeking his favor, reveals, in Him who is "the way, the truth, and the life," the *Right Way.* Having done this, it proceeds to regulate our intercourse with one another. Here, too, it opposes itself to the false maxims that govern the world at large, and pointedly denounces many errors which have become interwoven with the very texture of society. It shows us the glaring evils of that wrong way which is ordinarily practised, and reveals and inculcates the RIGHT WAY.

That RIGHT WAY it is the design of the present volume to unfold.

CHAPTER II.

DUTIES RELATING TO HUMAN INTERCOURSE.

I. LOVE TO OUR NEIGHBOR. The one great principle of the gospel, and one which is at the same time, "the fulfilling of the law," is *love*. This duty is variously expressed in the teachings of Christ and his apostles. Now it is called a love to our neighbor, now a love to the brethren, and now a love to enemies. It is represented under such names as "charity," "long-suffering," "meekness," "patience," "forbearance," "forgiveness," and "peace with all men." These different terms go to prove its universal character, and present some of its phases which might otherwise be overlooked by us. They each form a part of that "royal law" which embraces every duty of man to man, "*Thou shalt love thy neighbor as thyself.*" Matt. 22:39.

The best commentary upon this precept, is that afforded by its Author. In his beautiful parable of the "good Samaritan," our Lord for ever answers the question, "Who is my neighbor?" Luke 10:30–37. He there teaches us that an alien, and even an enemy, is our neighbor; that such an one, in distress, has a claim upon our compassionate, self-denying love; in short, that *every human being*, whoever and whatever he may be, has an undoubted right to our affection and our sympathy.

This demand may appear to some a severe one. What, it may be asked, must our affections go out as well to the stranger as to the intimate companion; to the inhabitant of a distant clime as well as to the beloved ones about us? Some may be disposed to scout such a requirement as absurd and impracticable. Let us, however, look for a moment at its justness.

What is it, we ask, that renders any human being an object of regard? It is the supposed existence of amiable qualities in the object, or else *the fact that there are certain natural ties between us.* Look, for instance, at the family. All must admit that the relations subsisting between its members afford a reason for the exercise of mutual affection between them. Applying this principle to mankind in general, will it not equally hold good? What is our race but one vast family, descended from a common parent, occupying a common home, similar in general character, tastes, and pursuits, and greatly dependent upon one another for the most ordinary comforts of life? "Have we not all one Father? hath not one God created us?" Mal. 2:10. It is both our fault and our misfortune that we have sadly lost sight of this relationship, and too frequently look for some conventional or social bond to regulate the outgoings of kindly feeling. As if God had implanted within us these fine affections for blessing only a select circle of chosen friends; or as if our hearts were incapable of embracing any more than a certain limited number of their fellow-hearts! Many live and act as if they had been gifted with but few and feeble affections, and were fearful of extending them too widely, lest they should all be lost. Yet so far from this being the case, it will be found true of our heart's wealth, as well as of our gold and silver, that "there is that scattereth, and yet increaseth; and there is that withholdeth more than is meet, but it tendeth to poverty." Prov. 11:24. We know not our own hearts, nor the powers of expansion with which God has endowed them. If men would but cultivate them, as they do their minds and bodies, they would prove capable of embracing in their large charities and sympathies, *all mankind.*

This required love is nowhere limited as to its *objects.* The gospel makes no distinctions, and not only does not exclude, but expressly includes the enemy, the persecutor, and the vile. We are to love not merely the friend, the benefactor, or the amiable, but the *fellow-mortal,* the *member of the human family.* And the reasons of this love are to be found not merely in favors received, or qualities admired, but in the divinely ordained relations of man to man, and in plain, simple duty, as prescribed in the gospel. To him who takes this high, scriptural view of his obligations, every man is in some degree an object of love. Upon seeing one who wears the human form in need of kindness, he unhesitatingly bestows it, stopping not to ask his name, his country, or his creed. He is *a man, and therefore a neighbor,* and his warm heart needs know no more to impel him to do his utmost to relieve and cheer him.

This "royal law" stops not with prescribing the objects of our love: it clearly defines its *measure.* It would be interesting to learn the precise guide which different minds would assign to regulate its strength. One would say, we must be governed by our own inclinations; another, by the deserts of the object; another, by his necessities. Never, in all the highest conceptions of human benevolence, would any have attained to the precept afforded by our Lord, "Thou shalt love thy neighbor *as thyself.*" He thus makes our self-love to be our guide in loving others. If ever at a loss to know how much of sympathy or regard we ought to cherish towards a fellow-man, our doubts may be removed by glancing within ourselves, and estimating the strength of that principle of self-love which we all to a greater or less degree possess. There is no danger that, with this for our standard, we shall exercise too large a charity for others. It may, however, be urged that a strict obedience to this precept is extremely difficult, if not impossible. This sad truth should only drive us to Him who has for us "fulfilled all righteousness." Yet the justness and obligation of a divine command does not depend upon our power literally to fulfil it. Are we absolved from the duty of loving God because we cannot love him with "*all*" our "heart," and "soul," and "strength," and "mind?"

As Christ has shown the objects and the measure of this love, so Paul has defined its *nature*. The word "charity," in the following passage, is strictly synonymous with *love*. "Charity suffereth long, and is kind; charity envieth not; charity vaunteth not itself, is not puffed up, doth not behave itself unseemly, seeketh not her own, is not easily provoked, thinketh no evil; rejoiceth not in iniquity, but rejoiceth in the truth; beareth all things, believeth all things, hopeth all things, endureth all things." 1 Cor. 13 : 4–7.

We have only to consider this LAW OF LOVE, and trace it to its consequences, to see that it tends inevitably to the preservation of harmony among men. They who honestly obey it will be linked together by a bond which even the widest diversities of sentiment, or the most provoking acts of injury cannot sever. Where this love is in the heart, the word. of resentment cannot linger upon the tongue, and the purpose of revenge, even if momentarily aroused, cannot ripen into deliberate action. The bitter retort that trembles on the lip gives place to the "soft answer," that "turneth away wrath;" and the flashing eye and menacing aspect are lost in the look of kindness and benevolence. The quarrel is avoided, hearts that were on the eve of sundering are knit yet more closely together, and love achieves the triumph over hatred, and right over wrong. This principle transforms the lion into the lamb, the vulture into the dove, the brutal, the degraded, and the unloving into beings all sympathy and tenderness, and all glowing with the noblest instincts of humanity. Where it has been deeply implanted by God's grace—and it is only there that it can fully and permanently abide—it assimilates man to the angels; nay, to Christ himself, who so loved us as to give himself for us, and to that Spirit whose richest fruits are "love" and "peace," and to God, who "is love."

Many theories have been invented by men for the world's regeneration. One plan after another, having for its object the perfection of our nature, has been in turn advanced and abandoned. Upon far higher than human authority, we present as the grand means for the elevation of our race, this LAW OF LOVE. It is only in proportion as men are governed by it, that they can arise to their true worth and dignity in the scale of being. For he who is not freed from the thraldom of angry passions, is little else than a slave; while he who is subject to this law of love, which is the law of liberty, has acquired the true self-mastery, and has attained, or is attaining the real nobility of man. To him, life is beautiful in its varied opportunities for kindness, and its numberless exercises of delightful affection. *Man* acquires a new interest in his eyes, and *God* becomes more than ever the object of happy contemplation; for he beholds mirrored in his own peaceful soul the loving smile of Jehovah, the author and true end of every benevolent emotion. Viewing this law, then, in all its length and breadth, as requiring love to God and man—to God first, and then through him and for him to man—it is to do more for the advancement of our race than all human means combined. As it becomes more and more prevalent, it will be found to effect, by its gradual workings, a thorough renovation of society. It will conquer pride, selfishness, and passion, uproot prejudice, disarm enmity and resentment, cause kind feelings and generous sympathies to animate every bosom, and conduct the world to its millennium of peace.

Such are to be, under God, the glorious results of a universal obedience to this law. It is for us to do our part towards hastening such a consummation, first, by conforming our own hearts and lives to it, and then by publishing it to others, as well by the power of a beautiful example, as by direct efforts. Every reader of this volume may thus become, in however humble a sphere, the means of extending the triumph of the gospel of peace.

II. Love to enemies. We have seen that the law of love applies as well to enemies as friends. Were there no special command upon the subject, we might still deduce from that general duty the particular one of loving our enemies and persecutors. To leave no room for doubt, however, it is urged in many distinct precepts, and occupies a prominent place in the religion of Jesus. In that epitome of religious duty, the sermon on the mount, our Lord says, "Ye have heard that it hath been said, Thou shalt love thy neighbor, and hate thine enemy; but I say unto you, *Love your enemies*," etc. Matt. 5:43, 44. This precept conveys to every candid mind but one signification. It can be understood in no other way than as exhorting us to check all feelings of resentment, and to cherish instead of them those of forbearance and good will. It stands opposed to all malice, enmity, and even bitterness of feeling; to an irascible disposition; to an unloving, unforgiving spirit; to the passionate retort, the hasty word of abuse or blow, the sullen, distant demeanor, and the deliberate persecution. It is equally plain, that to love an enemy is to cherish a hearty affection towards him, and to desire and seek his happiness. It is, as far as possible, to regard him with the same feelings, and treat him with the same kindness and consideration that we do our friends; to forgive his injurious conduct, and to aim at, and if possible, effect a reconciliation with him.

He who obeys this precept will fight, not against his adversary, but against his own rebellious heart, and will try to crush, not the offender, but those emotions of hatred or aversion with which he is tempted to regard him. He will studiously repress every feeling of anger, will subdue his countenance, his voice, his eye, his gestures, and his whole manner into the expression of tender regard, and will resolutely seal his lips against every utterance save a blessing or a prayer. He will try to behold in his antagonist a man, a brother, whom God bids him love; will charitably overlook his bad qualities, and seek out and admire his good ones, and will strive to discover, behind all his offences, something still deserving of his affection and sympathy.

The two precepts which we have now considered afford the fundamental principle of all others relating to human intercourse. As love is "the fulfilling of the law," so it alone can inspire an acceptable obedience to any of the precepts of the gospel. Let this be borne in mind as we now notice some of the required manifestations of that love. Let them be viewed as only the various streams of which love is the fountain, or as the diverging rays of which love is the central sun. By thus regarding them, we shall possess the clue to their meaning, and the secret of their fulfilment. With this general law clearly before us, the particular precepts of the gospel will develope harmoniously to our view, and we shall be the better fitted to comprehend and practise them.

CHAPTER III.

DUTIES RELATING TO HUMAN INTERCOURSE—CONTINUED.

III. FORGIVENESS. The question naturally occurs, how is the required love to enemies to be exhibited? What are the prescribed fruits and evidences of its existence? We learn from the teachings of Christ and his apostles, that one of the first and most important duties towards an offender is *forgiveness.*

In that prayer which our Lord has left on record for his disciples of every age, our forgiveness of one another is closely connected with that which we ask of God. He teaches us to pray, "Forgive us our debts, as we forgive our debtors." In order still further to impress our minds with its importance, he adds, "For, if ye forgive men their trespasses, your heavenly Father will also forgive you; but if ye forgive not men their trespasses, neither will your Father forgive your trespasses." Matt. 6 : 12, 14, 15. Of a similar import are the following: "If thy brother trespass against thee, rebuke him; and if he repent, forgive him. And if he trespass against thee seven times in a day, and seven times in a day turn again to thee, saying, I repent; thou shalt forgive him." Luke 17:3, 4. "Put on, therefore, as the elect of God, holy and beloved, bowels of mercies, kindness, humbleness of mind, meekness, long-suffering; forbearing one another, and forgiving one another, if any man have a quarrel against any: even as Christ forgave you, so also do ye." Col. 3:12, 13. "Be ye kind to one another, tender-hearted, forgiving one another, even as God for Christ's sake hath forgiven you." Eph. 4:32.

To forgive an offence is to overlook or remit it, and to regard and treat the offender as if he were not guilty. Such is the meaning that we attach to it in the petition, "Forgive us our debts," and such no doubt we must consider it when we add, "as we forgive our debtors." It is, as far as possible, to cherish towards an enemy such feelings, and so to conduct ourselves towards him as if he had not injured us. It is to treat him *as we would have God treat us.* Every Christian knows what is meant by forgiveness, as displayed by God towards the sinner. It means the same when exercised by man towards man, and implies the overlooking of an offence, the withholding of punishment from the offender, and the bestowment upon him of favors of which his conduct has rendered him seemingly unworthy.

This duty is not fulfilled by a merely outward reconciliation, nor by that absurd paradox with which some try to compromise between their religion and their anger—"I will forgive, but never forget." When truly cherished, it flows from the heart, and is a free, irrepressible manifestation of love to an enemy. Indeed, we have scriptural authority for regarding these two affections as identical, for the wise man says, "Love covereth all sins." Prov. 10:12. As the example of God is held up for our imitation in this respect, we may reasonably consider the nature of his forgiveness to be the standard of our own. Now what Christian would be willing to regard the divine pardon of his sins as a merely outward and formal one, or be contented to know that in the assurance, "Thy sins are forgiven thee," the words of God belie his heart? Is it not the joy of the redeemed that God "remits," "blots out," "forgets," and "hides his face from" their transgressions? These strong terms are held to be synonymous with forgiveness, and in them we find a sufficient guide to the meaning of the words, "forgiving one another, *even as God for Christ's sake hath forgiven you.*"

To forgive is not necessarily to encourage a wrong, nor even to pass it by in silence. Christ commands, "If thy brother trespass against thee, rebuke him." Every principle of virtue and morality demand that some kinds of trespass be pointedly denounced. This may be done in pity, in justice, and from a clear sense of duty, but never in anger or resentment.

Christ has clearly taught us the *extent* to which our forgiveness must be exercised. Peter once asked him, "How oft shall my brother sin against me, and I forgive him? till seven times? Jesus saith unto him, I say not unto thee, Until seven times: but, *Until seventy times seven.*" He then proceeds to illustrate this duty by the familiar parable of the forgiven and yet unforgiving debtor, who, failing to exhibit towards his fellow-servants the same compassion which he had just received, was "delivered to the tormentors." "So likewise," he adds, "shall my heavenly Father do also unto you, if ye from your hearts forgive not every one his brother their trespasses." Matt. 18 : 21–35. In these words we are taught that our forgiveness is to be *unlimited*, or is to be cherished, if it were possible, to as great a degree as God has manifested it towards us. We have only to attempt the measure of our offences against Him, and if we believe them all forgiven, we find before us an example far transcending the "seventy times seven."

He, therefore, who would be godlike will, when sinned against, instead of laying hands on the offender with the words, "Pay me that thou owest," be "moved with compassion, and loose him, and forgive him the debt." In order to dispose to this, he will view the error as leniently as possible, and will take into account the peculiar temperament and constitutional peculiarities of the trespassing brother, or those misfortunes which have perhaps soured his disposition, and rendered it thus unkindly. He will reflect that perhaps he was betrayed into his wrong conduct while in the heat of passion, and spoke or acted without deliberation, and soon will be all sorrow for his fault, and eager for forgiveness. He will bear in mind—how can he possibly forget it?—that he is daily making large drafts upon the divine forgiveness in the prayer, "Forgive us our debts, *as we forgive our debtors*," and the voice of Jesus will be heard and felt within him, saying, "If ye forgive not men their trespasses, neither will your Father forgive your trespasses."

The following incident, related of two Christions at Antioch, illustrates the important bearings of this virtue upon our state with God. Sapricius, who was a priest, and Nicephorus were at enmity. The latter plead earnestly for a reconciliation, which the former obstinately refused. Presently the persecution of Valerian began, and the priest, boldly confessing himself a Christian, was on his way to martyrdom. Nicephorus meeting him, again sued for forgiveness, but still in vain. At length, the one still pleading and the other refusing, they arrived together at the place of execution, where the priest, in order to save his life, made sudden shipwreck of his avowed faith, and abjured Christianity, and the other obtained the crown of martyrdom in his stead. The unforgiving servant was thus proved destitute of the divine pardon and grace, whatever may have been his professions to the contrary. He was not permitted to offer even the "gift" of himself upon the altar of Christian faith, because he obeyed not the Saviour's injunction, "first be reconciled to thy brother, and then come and offer thy gift." Matt. 5:24. An unforgiving spirit, however disguised, is an unchristian spirit. They who habitually cherish it, have cause to tremble lest they be startled from their fancied security by the words, "Oh, thou wicked servant, I forgave thee *all that debt* because thou desiredst me: shouldest not thou also have had compassion on thy fellow-servant, even as I had pity on thee?" And in the reward of the unforgiving one, who was "delivered to the tormentors," they may behold shadowed forth their own unhappy fate. "Blessed are the merciful, for they shall obtain mercy." Matt. 5:7. "He shall have judgment without mercy, that hath showed no mercy." James 2:13. "Forgive, and ye shall be forgiven." Luke 6:37.

IV. FORBEARANCE. Christ, in denouncing

the old maxim, "An eye for an eye, and a tooth for a tooth," exhorts, "*Resist not evil;* but whosoever shall smite thee on thy right cheek, turn to him the other also. And if any man will sue thee at the law, and take away thy coat, let him have thy cloak also. And whosoever shall compel thee to go a mile, go with him twain." Matt. 5:39–41. This duty is also urged in several other passages. "Love as brethren, be pitiful, be courteous: not rendering evil for evil, or railing for railing, but contrariwise blessing." 1 Peter 3:8, 9. "See that none render evil for evil unto any man; but ever follow that which is good, both among yourselves, and to all men." 1 Thess. 5:15. "Recompense to no man evil for evil." "Be not overcome of evil, but overcome evil with good." Rom. 12:17, 21. "Say not thou, I will recompense evil; but wait on the Lord, and he shall save thee." Prov. 20:22. "Walk worthy of the vocation wherewith ye are called, with all lowliness and meekness, with long-suffering, forbearing one another in love." Eph. 4:1, 2.

The ordinary usage of society opposes but a slight barrier to the exercise of revenge. Although the rule, "An eye for an eye, and a tooth for a tooth," may not literally be practised in civilized communities, it is *in spirit*, if not in letter, a fair expression of the public sentiment. Against this wrong principle Jesus opposes the precept, "*Resist not evil.*" Where love to an enemy exists in the heart, obedience to this requirement will follow as its fruit. The forgiveness of an offender implies a meek endurance of the offence. As God, when forgiving, stays his avenging arm, and withholds that punishment with which he might justly crush us, so those who would imitate him must endure injuries with forbearance and long-suffering. Those resentful thoughts and deeds which are generally regarded as the natural right of all, are not to be viewed with any favor by those who obey the gospel. The very word revenge should be blotted from their vocabulary, as, when the gospel triumphs, the thing itself shall be blotted from the world.

He, then, who would practise the right way, will prove his love and forgiveness by *resisting not injury*. As it is the part of love to suffer, rather than cause pain to its object, he will patiently endure wrong at the hands of another, and even rejoice in his enemy's exemption from it. Upon those occasions when some degree of resistance is necessary, he will offer it with reluctance, and instead of rejoicing at the opportunity for so doing, will deeply regret its necessity. As a general thing, he will meekly yield to the hand that smites and the tongue that reviles him, and will respond to the insult, or disprove the slander, more by his life than his words. Not only will he avoid the retaliatory blow, but even the witty sarcasm or inconsiderate jest, which would provoke a laugh at the expense of his adversary. The only resistance he will offer, will be to the evils of his own heart; and he will unite against them all those energies with which others are accustomed to resist an outward foe. Desirous of following "the things that make for peace," he will obey that voice of God, "Avenge not yourselves, but rather give place unto wrath: for it is written, Vengeance is mine; I will repay, saith the Lord." Rom. 12:19. "Blessed are the meek, for they shall inherit the earth." "Blessed are the peacemakers, for they shall be called the children of God." Matthew 5:5, 9.

V. RENDERING GOOD FOR EVIL. "*Love your enemies, bless them that curse you,* do good to them that hate you, and pray for them which despitefully use you and persecute you; that ye may be the children of your Father which is in heaven: for he maketh his sun to rise on the evil and on the good, and sendeth rain on the just and on the unjust." Matt. 5:44, 45. "Not rendering evil for evil, or railing for railing; but contrariwise blessing." 1 Pet. 3:9. "Bless them which persecute you; bless, and curse not." "Therefore, if thine enemy hunger, feed him; if he thirst, give him drink: for in so doing thou shalt heap coals of fire on his head." "Be not overcome of evil, but overcome evil with good." Rom. 12:14, 20, 21.

The meaning of these precepts is plain and undeniable. All must perceive that they forbid even a cold, distant demeanor towards an enemy, or a disregard of his interests. Some think that they have carried their kindness quite far enough when they have allowed the trespasser to *go unharmed.* But we are here taught that we may not even treat with "silent contempt" him whom duty forbids us to punish in any other way; and that while endeavoring to forgive and forbear, we are not absolved from the further obligation to associate with and benefit him.

To those who acknowledge the wisdom and obligation of this class of precepts, little need be said as to the manner of their fulfilment. Circumstances will generally determine the mode in which they may be the best obeyed, and suggest the particular kind of good which it is our duty to render. Where the right disposition exists, opportunities for exercising it will not be wanting. Paul has specified two extreme cases—yet with no design of excluding those of lesser importance—in the exhortation, "If thine enemy hunger, feed him; if he thirst, give him drink." The meaning of this is, that rather than rejoice in his sufferings of any kind whatever, we should relieve them. In the divine example—which we should ever look upon as our standard—God, who is infinite, blesses those of his enemies who have a heart to accept his gifts, with infinite good. He does not discriminate between the very gross and the comparatively slight offender, but bestows upon all who will receive it in his appointed way the same forgiveness, the same salvation, and the same heaven. So we, in doing good to those who hate us, are not to be governed by their deserts, but by our opportunities for benefiting them, and their willingness to be benefited by us.

He who obeys these precepts will mark every occasion of injury by the bestowment of some peculiar favor, so that it may be said of him, as it was of Archbishop Cranmer, "The best way to make him your friend is to do him an ill turn." If he can discover no necessity to be supplied, he will at least bestow the kind word, and exhibit in look and demeanor, and in those numberless acts of courtesy which it is always in our power to render, a sincere desire for his welfare. Every repetition of the offence will be the signal for repeated kindnesses; and even should this strife be long continued, he will be as eager to follow every evil with good to the end, as was ever an angry disputant to secure the "last word" of a controversy.

He will especially delight in praying for his enemy. And here, after all, is the noblest triumph of good over evil; for what blessing can surpass that of earnest prayer in behalf of a fellow-creature? By means of it we not only exercise and put in practice our own love to him, but, if our prayers are what they should be, we enlist *God* in the work of benefiting him, and obtain for him such favors as no mortal could confer. Perhaps, in answer to our effectual prayer, a soul is saved, new joy caused in heaven over a repenting sinner, and he who cursed us blessed with "a crown of life," and "an eternal weight of glory." Such is said to have been the result of a poor negro's prayer, once offered in behalf of a cruel and ungodly master. He was a slave, and had been severely whipped for reading the Bible. Soon afterwards, his master going near the place of punishment, his attention was arrested by the voice of one engaged in prayer. As he listened, out of mere curiosity, he heard the poor slave imploring God to forgive the injustice of his master, to touch his heart with a sense of his sin, and to make him a good Christian. Struck with remorse, he made an immediate change in his life, which had been careless and dissipated, burnt his profane books and cards, provided for the liberation of all his slaves, and appeared now to study only how to render his wealth and talents useful to others. Who could desire to bestow or to receive a richer blessing than is hinted at in the words, "Pray for them that despitefully use you and persecute you?"

VI. THE GOLDEN RULE. It only remains that we notice one more precept upon this subject, namely, that commonly and justly known as "the *golden rule*." In his sermon upon the mount, Christ gives us the sum of "the law and the prophets," with regard to the relative duties of men, in the words, "*Therefore all things whatsoever ye would that men should do to you, do ye even so to them.*" Matt. 7 : 12.

This precept embraces in its meaning every other relating to human intercourse. It demands love to all men, including enemies, the forgiveness of injuries, the rendering of good for evil, and every duty of man to man which is enjoined in the gospel. It is the exact counterpart of the command, "Thou shalt love thy neighbor as thyself," the only difference between them being this, that while the one prescribes the disposition to be cherished, the other points out the manner in which that disposition is to be exhibited.

This rule is equally applicable to every relation in life, and to every individual. Christ makes no exception, and we can make none. Indeed, he teaches us that in the word "men," as here employed, enemies are expressly included. In Luke's account of this command, it is immediately followed by these words, "For if ye love them which love you, what thank have ye? for sinners also love those that love them. And if ye do good to them which do good to you, what thank have ye? for sinners also do even the same." "But *love ye your enemies*, and do good and lend, hoping for nothing again; and your reward shall be great, and ye shall be the children of the Highest: for he is kind unto the unthankful and to the evil. Be ye therefore merciful, as your Father also is merciful." Luke 6 : 32–36.

Now what is the treatment of an enemy that is here prescribed? Suppose an injured person is striving honestly to act upon this rule—his reflections will be such as these: "Placing my soul in his soul's stead, how should I desire to be treated by one whom I had thus injured? Should I be made happy by his retaliation? Should I not prefer to be met with a meek, quiet demeanor, with words and deeds of love, and a spirit eager to forgive and bless me? As, then, I should wish thus to be treated, so I will now love, forgive, and bless my adversary. As I would that he should do unto me, even so, God helping me, I will do to him."

It is easy to see what would be the necessary results of a general obedience to this precept. It would effectually curb the most violent dispositions. It would banish from the world every form of strife, for it would nip in their beginnings all hatred and ill-will. There would then be no occasion for the command, "Resist not evil," for evil would not be inflicted by man upon his fellow. Resentment would be unknown, for there would be no injuries to resent. The universal observance of this rule would clothe social intercourse with a new and holy charm, and cause all distractions, altercations, and wars, to cease from among men.

Such are some of the precepts given in the gospel for the government of human intercourse. Beautiful in their simplicity, wise in their adaptations, perfect in their binding power, and glorious in their tendencies, they prove themselves divine. They come to us all glowing with the spirit of their Author, and clothed with a loveliness which cannot but attract, and a majesty and authority which command our reverent homage. Truly, "never man spake like this man!" And they are no merely sublime theories, to be rather distantly admired than obeyed, but near, living, and practical. They may be made the means of blessing in every relation to which they are applied; and while strengthening and sweetening the bonds of love, extend them far and wide. In these precepts is clearly enough revealed the *Right Way*. It is for us joyfully to accept and obey them as a sufficient rule of duty.

He who fulfils them from the heart will have obtained a glorious conquest over both himself and his adversary: over himself, because he will have effectually resisted those passions which most enslave us; and over his adversary, because, even if he does not conquer him by kindness, he at least obtains the mastery in the maintenance of self-possession and manly dignity of character. His is the sublime consciousness of duty performed and good conferred, and not the scathing remembrance of his own sin, and its bitter fruit in another's misery.

His is the true honor, and whether acknowledged by men or not, a glory far surpassing that which encircles the names of many whom the world calls heroes. His is the highest wisdom, for "he that is slow to wrath is of great understanding," Prov. 14 : 29, and "the wisdom that is from above is first pure, then peaceable, gentle, and easy to be entreated." Jas. 3 : 17. He approves himself *a man* in the highest and truest sense of the term, for he exhibits something of that image of God in which man was first created, and which it is the design of the gospel to restore. By the very exercise of these kindly feelings, and by the grace which prompts them, he rises to a higher sphere of existence, where he breathes a purer air, and basks more fully in the rays of the divine sun of life and blessedness. He lives the true life of humanity, and in his obedience to the "royal law" of love, walks a king among his fellows. The tyrants Hate, Envy, Malice, and Revenge, who keep so many millions groaning under their servitude, lie humbled at his feet, their power weakened, if not wholly broken, and he who was once their degraded victim is made their master; while the mild virtues, Love, Forgiveness, Patience, and Good-will, habitually sway his thoughts and actions, and gild his whole outer and inner life with their holy lustre.

CHAPTER IV.

OBJECTIONS AND DIFFICULTIES CONSIDERED.

It is to be expected that precepts such as we have now considered, will encounter much opposition. As they directly conflict with the commonly received maxims of society, as well as with the principles of our depraved nature, it is not to be wondered at that men raise many objections to them, and shrink from the real or imagined difficulties of their practice.

I. It may be objected to the gospel method of intercourse, that *honor requires that every insult or injury be resented.* It may be urged that he who obeys the gospel will be branded by many as cowardly and mean-spirited.

There have been different notions of honor among different nations; and every age has had its peculiar ideas upon the subject. In ancient Sparta, successful theft was considered honorable. In parts of India, it is at this day thought disgraceful for a widow to survive her husband. It is said of the Japanese, that upon occasion of gross insult the offended person is bound in honor to commit suicide by disembowelling himself with his sword. In modern times, Fashion has, in some places, demanded that men deliberately shoot one another, as the only honorable mode of settling their disputes. Happily this relic of barbarism is fast disappearing from civilized communities, and in most portions of them the duellist is justly regarded as brutal, degraded, and murderous. Still, it is very generally considered an essential qualification of a brave man that he in some way resent injuries. He who meekly yields to them, or repays them with blessings, is apt to be suspected of cowardice; while he whose blood boils with indignation against an adversary, and who retorts his scurrilous abuse, or passionately chastises him, is admired as "a man of spirit." Even if, in an uncontrollable outburst of wrath, he kills his foe, many are disposed to look leniently upon the criminal, and instead of punishing his *crime*, merely to commiserate his *misfortune*.

These ideas of honor are as false and unworthy as those we have just noticed. He who pleads them, proceeds on precisely the same principle that demands the Hindoo suttee, or the Japanese suicide: namely, that popular opinion is the true standard of glory. But what is its true standard? It is afforded only in the word of God, and the example of Christ. Our Maker, in revealing to us his will and his glory, has also revealed both our happiness and our glory, for they coincide. The divine word teaches us that "it is an honor for a man to cease from strife," Prov. 20:3; that "he that is slow to anger is better than the mighty; and he that ruleth his spirit, than he that taketh a city," Prov. 16:32; that "the discretion of a man deferreth his anger; and it is his glory to pass over a transgression." Prov. 19:11.

What is it that constitutes honor? Is it victory? Then the more arduous the conquest, the higher the honor. If a surmounting of the greatest obstacles, and an achieving of victory in the face of the most violent opposition, be glory, then that term is not so applicable to the conqueror of men as to the conqueror of *himself*. The fiery duellist and the successful general are esteemed courageous; yet many a meek and lowly Christian, who is called mean-spirited by those whom he forgives, and who is now unknown to human fame, but whose name shines brightly in the book of life, far surpasses them in the splendor of his achievements. Again, is honor the supremacy of mind or matter, of soul or body? That brute is a distinguished one who is the terror of his fellows, and so is that man; but is his an enviable distinction? Is that a worthy vindication of personal honor which consists in the exhibition of base, brutal qualities; or that which shows a triumph of reason and good sense? Surely none need hesitate as to whether he will aim at the honor of a brute, or that of an intelligent, reasoning man.

They who are accustomed to stand punctiliously upon this imaginary point of honor, are so far from being honorable, that they are little else than abject slaves. The spirit which will not yield to an outward injury marks plainly a state of inward servitude. The "soft answer" and the forbearing and forgiving conduct mark those noble beings who have struggled into manly liberty, and who, fearless of custom, popular opinion, and false honor—those scourges with which our passions lash us to obedience—stand up erect in their lofty heroism, their own masters, and servants only to their Maker.

Every consideration of honor and self-respect, then, so far from affording any objection to the right way, furnishes the most powerful motives to its practice. Thus, we are authorized to hope, it shall yet be considered by the world at large. The time is coming—all prophecy, and all the current of human progress alike point to it—when the false judgments of bygone generations shall be reversed; when the bloody deeds of heroes shall be stripped of their fictitious splendor; when public opinion, moulded by the sweet influences of the gospel of peace, shall frown upon all exhibitions of resentment; when the niche in Fame's temple, which only slaves to passion are now allowed to fill, shall be occupied by the most meek, most loving, and most forgiving of men; and when the peaceful virtues shall render their possessors glorious. Towards this change of public sentiment events are rapidly tending. We appeal to the reader whether he will retard it by conforming to views which all reason and scripture pronounce erroneous; or whether he will hasten it, by seeking, in noble independence of the world's false notions, *true glory*.

II. It may be objected to the gospel method,

that there are *aggravated cases of injury*, to which it is not applicable. Admitting its justness with reference to the ordinary and lesser occasions of strife, is there not "a point, beyond which forbearance ceases to be a virtue?" It may be said, I am willing to forgive *slight* injuries; but there are those of a graver character, which must not be overlooked. Such, for instance, are deliberate persecutions, long persisted in, and marked with constant efforts for my ruin. The sum of the objection would amount to this: "The principle of the right way is good—it is divine; but the extent to which it is to be practised *is in an inverse ratio to the enormity of the offence*. The greater the injury, the less it is to be forgiven. If an enemy hate me but little, I am to love him; if a great deal, I am justified in hating him."

Those who make use of this objection, either widely mistake the character of the gospel precepts, or do not obey them at all; for they have a direct reference to the grosser and more aggravated kinds of trespass; and in this fact lies their chief value. Peter says, "For this is thankworthy, if a man for conscience toward God endure grief, *suffering wrongfully*. For what glory is it, if, when ye be buffeted for your faults, ye shall take it patiently? but if, when ye do well, and suffer for it, ye take it patiently, this is acceptable with God." 1 Pet. 2 : 19, 20. If love, meekness, and forgiveness be duties, the fact that the injury is severe and undeserved, so far from absolving us from them, only demands that they be the more thoroughly and earnestly discharged.

This objection is put at rest by the example of those who are held up in the Scriptures for our imitation. The case of the martyr Stephen was surely an aggravated one, for his enemies were stoning him to death. Yet he did not deem this a sufficient reason for cherishing one bitter feeling towards them, but prayed with his last breath, "Lord, lay not this sin to their charge." Acts 7 : 60. What grosser indignities can be imagined than those that were heaped upon Christ? Betrayed, scourged, spit upon, crucified—not all this accumulation of injuries could extort from him a whisper of resentment, or prevent his firm, hearty utterance of the prayer, "Father, forgive them!" Who can estimate the enormity of every sinner's offences against God? Are they not a thousand-fold more aggravated than any we can commit against one another? Yet hear God saying, "Though your sins be as scarlet, they shall be as white as snow; though they be red like crimson, they shall be as wool." Isa. 1:18. Here is our standard. When we are required to exercise a forgiveness and long-suffering greater than these, it will be time enough to hesitate; but let not those who are daily the objects of a forbearance so great that only God could exercise it, attempt nicely to assign the limit beyond which "forbearance ceases to be a virtue," and hate to be a crime. We are not warranted in the belief that there is any such limit. The maxim just quoted was never derived from God's word, nor from the example of God or Christ.

III. Another and plausible objection to the right way is, that *its practice would only subject us to yet greater injuries.*

Whether this is true or not, the fact that it is our duty sufficiently answers this, as indeed it does every objection. We have no right to make the real or supposed results of a divine obligation the criterion of our obedience. If the way which we have presented is the *right* way, it is our plain duty to follow it, *whatever be the consequences.* The objection, however, has not the sanction of either reason or revelation. Obedience to the gospel must necessarily lessen strife, and "turn away wrath." He who controls his own passions, acquires thereby a mastery over those of his adversary, and by his very forbearance disarms the other's enmity, and recalls him to reflection. He does indeed outwardly yield, in refraining from physical resistance, yet he subdues him by a moral power which is far more effective than that of the strongest arm, or the deadliest weapon.

But it may be said, while this is in general true, it is not always the case. When assailed by one of violent temper, will not our forbearance be abused? Are there not those who will basely take advantage of it, and improve the opportunity thus afforded them, by new injuries? It is the misfortune of the Christian world that this has been so generally taken for granted, that few have fairly tested the question in their own experience. Men have so believed their fears upon this subject, that they have rarely given themselves the opportunity to learn whether those fears are just, or groundless. Even the best of Christians have been slow to believe that He who commands is able to protect his children in their obedience. But is he not the God of providence? How easy it would be for him to avert the blow that is aimed at a faithful disciple, to wither the arm that is lifted against him, and instantly to subdue the ferocious tiger to the disposition of the lamb! We are accustomed, in regard to other duties, to expect that God will sustain and defend us in their discharge. It is a sad *want of faith* which prevents us from thus relying upon him in the fulfilment of these. When that faith shall be more strongly cherished, it will be found to fulfil our highest expectations; and it will be seen that by the operation of natural laws, and the ordinary course of divine Providence, the right way results only in good to those who practise it. This, the known character of God, and the very constitution of his moral government, lead us confidently to believe.

Owing to the general distrust upon this subject, and to the few efforts made to obey these precepts, we cannot point to as many proofs of the security of the right way as might be desired. There have been instances, however, in which its fearless practice has been rewarded by exemption from imminent peril. One of the most beautiful and affecting of these is related of David, 1 Sam. chap. 24. He had been for a long time pursued by Saul, who was eager to take his life. From place to place his enemy had hunted him like a wild beast, but without success. At length, having been informed that he was in the wilderness of Engedi, he went there with three thousand men, intent upon his capture and destruction. While upon this mission of hate, he providentially turned aside into a cave in which David and his men had concealed themselves, and there slept. Here was an excellent opportunity for David to rid himself of his foe. He might have reasoned thus: "My life is in peril. If I now slay him, I shall thereby save myself. If I permit him to live, will he not employ the life which I spare in compassing my destruction? Will not my forbearance expose me to yet greater injuries?" His sense of duty, however, prevailed over his fears, and he contented himself with cutting off the skirt of Saul's garment, for an evidence that he had been within his power; although even for this his heart afterwards "smote him." When Saul had arisen and departed, David followed him, presented himself before him, and assured him of his kind feelings and desire for his welfare. What was the result? Did that bitterest of foes seize this opportunity to gratify his hatred? No; the fiery enemy suddenly became the humble suppliant. Melted with contrition, "Saul lifted up his voice and wept," and said to David, "thou art more righteous than I, for thou hast rewarded me good, whereas I have rewarded thee evil; . . . . wherefore the Lord reward thee good for that thou hast done unto me this day." He then predicted David's future triumph and royalty, implored his mercy towards himself and his seed, and went home without so much as lifting a finger against him for whose blood he had so long thirsted.

There have been many other instances in which a similar treatment of enemies has resulted in a like manner. These have principally occurred among a class who have been the most conspicuous, in modern times, for their obedience to these precepts—the *Friends*, or Quakers. Most nobly have they exemplified and vindicated them. Embodying them as a distinct and prominent feature of their creed, and accepting their most literal interpretation, they have boldly put them in practice upon the most trying occasions. The remarkable success which has attended their efforts, is a sufficient answer to the objection under consideration. Well will it be for the church and the world, when all Christians shall heed the lesson which has thus, for two centuries, been practically unfolding before them.

During the Irish rebellion of 1798, the peace principles of the Quakers were put to the severest test. Viewed with suspicion by both parties, and threatened and insulted upon all sides, they yet had the courage publicly to destroy every weapon among them, and firmly adhered to their resolution to do good to both parties, and harm to neither. It is a remarkable circumstance that throughout that fierce and bloody struggle, these peacemakers were generally uninjured. However wild and reckless may have been the fury of either party when victorious, their cry was, "Spare the Quakers; they have done good to all, and harm to none." Their peace principles afforded them an equal protection in their intercourse with the savage tribes of North America. It is a well-known and significant fact, that during the early settlement of this country, they were generally exempted from the hostile attacks of the Indians. Of this the history of the colony of Pennsylvania affords a striking example.

It is related of Robert Barclay, that he was once attacked by a highwayman, a pistol levelled at him, and a demand made for his purse. Calm and self-possessed, he looked the robber in the face, and mildly assured him that he was his and every man's friend, and willing to relieve his wants; but being free from the fear of death, he was not to be intimidated by a deadly weapon. He then appealed to him whether he could have the heart to shed the blood of one who had no other feeling or purpose but to do him good. "The robber was confounded; his eye suffused with tears; his brawny arm trembled; his pistol fell to his side; and he fled, abashed, from the presence of the hero who had dared to 'resist not evil.'"

During a violent persecution of Christians in France, in the early part of the last century, M. de St. Claude, a man of eminent piety, was imprisoned in the Bastile. At the same time a man was confined there who was such a monster of ferocity that no one dared to approach him. He seldom spoke without the most horrid blasphemies, and violently struck all who came near him. After exhausting every expedient to overcome this brutal disposition, the governor of the prison persuaded Claude to undertake the task. He was shut up with the inhuman wretch, who at first abated none of his violence, but constantly assailed him with angry revilings and savage blows. The humble Christian responded to them with mild, forgiving words, and patient endurance, and prayers. Such a warfare could not long be sustained. The monster was conquered. Looking in the face of his companion, he cast himself at his feet, and embracing them, burst into a flood of tears. He implored Claude's forgiveness, and entreated him to teach him that religion which had influenced him to such noble conduct. He became from that time a meek, peaceable, and pious man; and even when restored to liberty, it was with difficulty that he was persuaded to leave his Christian friend.

We do not affirm that such would be the invariable result of obeying the gospel precepts. It is, however, *the general tendency of that obedi-*

ence. Instances have occurred in which forbearance has been attended with consequences precisely opposite. The lives of the Christian martyrs, and especially that of the divinely forgiving, and yet crucified Jesus, show that love will not always disarm an enemy. But that such will be its ordinary effect seems reasonable, and is confirmed by human experience. At all events, those who make use of this objection should try the experiment of the prescribed course of conduct, before positively asserting its insecurity. It has never yet been sufficiently tested, nor will it be, until Christians shall awake from their long indifference, and in the exercise of a simple faith in God, try to discharge plain duty. They will then discover that in this, as in every other respect, duty is interest, and that the Right Way is the only safe way of conducting social intercourse. "Who is he that will harm you, if ye be followers of that which is good?" 1 Peter, 3:13. "When a man's ways please the Lord, he maketh even his enemies to be at peace with him." Prov. 16:7. "Say not thou, I will recompense evil; but wait on the Lord, and he shall save thee." Prov. 20:22.

IV. Perhaps the most formidable objection to the gospel method, is *the difficulties which attend its practice.*

Some of these have been alluded to. The chief one, however, and that which lies at the foundation of all the rest, is the opposition it encounters in our own bosoms. It may be said with truth, "The duties urged upon us run directly counter to our natural dispositions. Whether it be our fault or our misfortune, we are born into the world with certain propensities which clamor earnestly for gratification. Such are anger, resentment, and the desire of resisting evil; and to act contrary to them would be to revolutionize every instinct and impulse of our nature." But consider,

1. *Of what religious duty may not the same thing be said?* The impenitent may object, with equal justness, that repentance is very hard; and the unbeliever, that faith in Christ is unnatural to him, and exceedingly difficult of attainment. Every sinner may urge, with truth, that his heart is strongly averse to loving and serving God. Of what path of revealed duty do not timid pilgrims say, "There are lions in the way?" He who stops to count the cost of

a religious life, will find many a "hill Difficulty" intervening between him and the celestial city. Yet thousands of Christians have bravely surmounted them all; and the whole church militant is made up of those who are grappling with and conquering difficulties as vast as any that oppose our obedience to these precepts. Let us place them upon a level with many other duties, such as love to God, repentance, faith, holiness; and ask, will not the objection apply equally to them? Must not the objector, to be consistent, give up all religion, and refuse to obey any of the divine precepts?

2. Great as may be the difficulties in the way, *experience has shown that they may be overcome.* Every reader can probably call to mind some trophy of divine grace, in whom the most resentful dispositions have been rooted out, and a heart of love and forgiveness implanted in their stead. Saul, the fierce, impetuous persecutor, "breathing out threatenings and slaughter against the disciples of the Lord," was afterwards enabled to say, "Being reviled, we bless; being persecuted, we suffer it; being defamed, we entreat." Compare Acts 9 : 1, and

1 Cor. 4:12, 13. The dying prayer of Christ-like Stephen was, "Lord, lay not this sin to their charge." Acts 7:60. It is said that James the less, who suffered a martyrdom similar to that of Stephen, prayed for his murderers amid a shower of stones which they cast at him, until one of them beat out his brains with a fuller's club. The history of the church of God, and especially that of the Christian martyrs, furnishes numberless other instances of the practical fulfilment of the precepts, "Love your enemies, bless them that curse you," etc. They therefore have been obeyed; and what should prevent their fulfilment by every Christian?

This objection, however plausible in the mouth of the ungodly, comes with an ill grace from the Christian. For, does it not argue a sad want of confidence in that almighty Power from whence he professes to derive all his sufficiency? It reveals, too, a glaring inconsistency of religious practice; for it virtually assumes that while divine grace can strengthen for some kinds of duty, there are others for which it is inadequate; or that while it can enable us to repent and believe, it cannot enable us to love our enemies, and forgive injuries. What wonder is it, if those who thus practically distrust their Maker, should be left to feel their weakness, and be overcome by those difficulties which they do not rightly seek to subdue? Let them, however, lean upon that arm which is stretched out for their assistance, and the obstacles will vanish from this, as they do from every other path of duty.

CHAPTER V.

MOTIVES TO THE RIGHT WAY.

While there are no objections which can reasonably be urged against the *right way* of conducting intercourse, there are many strong *motives* to its practice.

I. One of the least of these is, that *personal policy demands it.* This, of itself, were an unworthy motive to the discharge of any duty; yet it is perhaps proper to notice it in connection with others which we shall present.

All must have observed, in the ordinary dealings of men, the power that resides in a bland, courteous demeanor. Whatever be the object to be gained, whether friends, pleasures, honors, or riches, those are the most successful who are uniformly polite, and considerate of others' happiness. A smile, or a kind word, will often accomplish more in a person's favor than the most masterly stroke of cunning. In business transactions, the man who controls his passions has by far the advantage of him who does not. A resentful disposition excites distrust, wherever it is known. Prudent men avoid those who exhibit it, and in all their dealings give the preference to those of mild temper, and accustomed to self-command. Alexander the Great, amid all his bloody conquests, recognized the importance of a kind treatment of both friends and enemies, as the best means of furthering his ambitious schemes. Being asked how he had been able at so early an age and in so short a period to conquer such vast regions, and establish so great a name, he replied, "I used my enemies so well that I compelled them to become my friends, and I treated my friends with such constant regard that they became unalterably attached to me." Were there no other and loftier aim in life than *success*, every consideration of sound policy would demand the cultivation of a kind, forbearing, and forgiving disposition. We may add to this the motive of *personal safety*. The conduct required of us, so far from exposing to yet greater injury, is our best safeguard against it. Resistance to wrong generally provokes to its repetition. The irritable and impetuous are of all men the most liable to be trespassed against; while they who return good for evil convert their enemies into friends, and make them minister to their happiness. So far, then, as regards the accomplishment of the most selfish ends, such as our own aggrandizement, and personal security, the right way is "the best policy."

II. We urge as another motive, *our own liability to offend, and our frequent need of forgiveness from others.*

Who is there that is not sometimes off his guard, and liable to be surprised into an offence against a fellow-man? What tongue is so bridled as not, at times, unjustly to assail and injure others? They who make the highest attainments in the religious life are forced to confess, of their relations both to God and man, "In many things we offend all."

This undeniable fact should have great weight with us in our dealings with mankind. He who allows it its proper influence, will, upon every occasion of injury from another, reflect that he may yet need the kind forbearance of that very individual. He will reason with himself thus: "What am *I*, that I should resent an offence, or withhold forgiveness from a brother? When I have done hating, it will be time enough to refuse to love; when I have done sinning, time enough to be unforgiving; when I do no evil, time enough to resist evil; and when I need not the kind deeds and prayers of others, time enough to withhold them from any. Until then, I will be consistent with myself, and forgive, as I would be forgiven either of God or man." Such is a reasonable view of the subject, and such are the thoughts and resolutions which best become us. The resentful man, while of all others the most likely to give offence, is the very last who ought to do so. For he cannot reasonably exact a treatment which he refuses to render; and he has no right to complain if all his injurious words and actions are promptly retaliated. On the other hand, he who, conscious of his frailty, cherishes a spirit of meekness and long-suffering, may with greater reason hope to be met with the same spirit. Our own interests therefore, no less than a manly consistency of conduct, demand that we extend to those injuring us that forgiveness which we ourselves may require.

III. Another motive may be drawn from *the close connection which exists between our forgive-*

ness of one another, and that which we need from God.

Our Lord, after teaching his disciples to pray, "Forgive us our debts as we forgive our debtors," adds as the reason of that petition, "For if ye forgive men their trespasses, your heavenly Father will also forgive you; but if ye forgive not men their trespasses, neither will your Father forgive your trespasses." Matt. 6 : 14, 15. While we are not to understand by these words that the exercise of forgiveness is of itself a procuring cause of the divine pardon, yet they clearly teach us that it is one of those holy dispositions which are *essential to saving piety*. It is one of the most beautiful fruits of Christian faith and love, and an indispensable part of true religion. So closely is it connected with every other Christian grace, that its absence argues the absence of other characteristics of genuine piety. Those who habitually fail to cherish it are still under the divine condemnation. They may loudly protest their faith in Christ, but their claims to religion are proved groundless by the fact that it does not inspire a forgiveness of the erring.

What a solemn thought, and how full of suggestion to the professed follower of Christ! No earthly blessing can be compared, in the believer's estimation, with the divine forgiveness, neither can any thing compensate for its loss. It is the broad, firm basis upon which is built the whole edifice of his Christian hopes and consolations. To be destitute of this is to be destitute of them all, and be left to perish under the burden of unpardoned guilt, and the crushing weight of the "wrath to come." They who are aware of a tithe of the blessings for which they ask in the prayer, "Forgive us our debts," will perceive that it is no ordinary motive to forgiveness that is here held out.

A fellow-passenger of John Wesley in his voyage to America, after relating to him a provocation which he had just received from his servant, said, "I will be revenged on him. The rascal should have taken care how he used me so, *for I never forgive.*" "Then I hope, sir," replied Wesley, "*you never sin.*" The rebuke was a just one, and will apply with equal force to all who cherish a similar spirit. He whose heart is closed in frequent resentment against his fellow-men, must expect that the heart of God will be closed against his entreaties; while he whose heart expands with love to all men, and who receives his trespassing brother to its cordial embrace, and then prays, "Forgive us our debts *as we forgive our debtors,*" may hopefully listen for the voice of his pardoning Father, "Son, be of good cheer; *thy sins be forgiven thee.*" "With the merciful, thou wilt show thyself merciful." Psa. 18:25. "With what judgment ye judge, ye shall be judged; and with what measure ye mete, it shall be measured to you again." Matt. 7 : 2.

IV. Another motive to the right way may be drawn from *its happy influence upon the cause of Christianity.*

To those who are acquainted with the requirements of the gospel, the frequent practice of Christians appears grossly inconsistent. The infidel narrowly scans the conduct of the church with reference to her acknowledged duties, and pronounces her professions sincere or otherwise in the proportion in which she discharges them. He reads the divine code by which we say that we are guided, and turning from it to our actual conduct, defies us to point to its fulfilment. He eagerly adopts the maxim of holy writ, "By their fruits ye shall know them," and arguing from evident discrepancies between profession and practice, impresses his fiendish principles upon many a doubting mind. How shall such arguments be met and refuted? Only by *a practical conformity to our acknowledged standard, the word of God.* Let Christians be consistent with their professions, be actuated by the enlarged charity which is required of them, and exhibit on every occasion the spirit of love and forbearance, and their simple discharge of known duty will be the means of rearing such a bulwark of defence that "the gates of hell shall not prevail against" them. So doing, they will wipe away a reproach which has long adhered to them, and remove many a stumbling-block from the path of the ungodly.

Such a course of conduct would also advance the interests of Christianity, *by its exhibition to others of the most beautiful traits of true religion.* As a missionary was once preaching in a chapel to a crowd of Hindoos, a strong native aimed a blow at him from behind the desk, intending to knock him down. Happily, it fell on his shoulders, and did him but little injury. The hearers, however, enraged at the offender, seized him, and secured his person. "Now, what shall I do with him?" asked the missionary. "Give him a good beating," said some. "Send him to the judge," cried others, "and he will receive two years' hard labor on the roads." "I cannot follow your advice," he replied. "My religion commands me to love my enemies, and to do good to those who treat me injuriously." Then addressing the culprit, he said, "I forgive you from my heart; but never forget that you owe your escape from punishment to that Jesus whom you persecuted in me." The effect of this scene upon the Hindoos is described as having been most impressive. "They saw it and marvelled; and unable longer to keep silence, they sprang on their feet and shouted, 'Victory to Jesus Christ! Victory to Jesus Christ!'" The general exhibition of such a spirit would do much towards placing religion in its true light before the world, as in every way lovely and attractive, and as eminently practical, and adapted to the wants of society. It would go far towards achieving throughout the earth the victory which it accomplished in the Indian mission chapel, "*Victory to Jesus Christ!*"

V. Another powerful motive to these duties is afforded by *the divine example.*

This is made use of by our Saviour in his sermon upon the mount. After exhorting, "Love your enemies," etc., he adds as the reason of his exhortation, "That ye may be the children of your Father which is in heaven; for he maketh his sun to rise on the evil and on the good, and sendeth rain on the just and on the unjust." Matt. 5:45. In closing this branch of his precepts, he says, "Be ye therefore perfect, even as your Father which is in heaven is perfect." Matt. 5:48. In several other passages, God is thus held up as our pattern: "Be ye therefore merciful, as your Father also is merciful." Luke 6:36. "Be ye kind one to another, tender-hearted, forgiving one another, even as God for Christ's sake hath forgiven you." Eph. 4:32. "Be ye therefore followers of God as dear children." Eph. 5:1.

In this, as in every other respect, God is the example of his people. It is the part of his children to study carefully his spirit and conduct, and aim at the closest conformity to it. What is that spirit and conduct? *Let the experience of all the ungodly answer.* They abuse his mercies, spurn his offers of forgiveness, and despise, reject, and crucify his Son. How does the insulted Jehovah respond to such treatment? Does he whet his "glittering sword," and his "hand take hold on judgment?" Thus he might justly do; but, instead of it, he forbears and entreats, and "all day long" stretches forth his hands "unto a disobedient and gainsaying people;" still calls, although men refuse, still stretches out his hand, although no man regards it. See Rom. 10:21, and Prov. 1:24. "He hath not dealt with us after our sins, nor rewarded us according to our iniquities." Psa. 103:10. "It is of the Lord's mercies that we are not consumed, because his compassions fail not." Lam. 3:22. What spirit does God manifest? *Let the experience of the forgiven sinner answer.* With the cry of David, "Mine iniquities are gone over my head: as a heavy burden they are too heavy for me;" and with the prayer, "God be merciful to me a sinner," he has bowed before his Maker, and obtained the free pardon of his crimes, and the blessing of eternal life. The whole tenor of God's dealings with our race exhibits a forbearance so great, and a long-suffering so protracted, that no words can adequately express it. We can only say of it, *it is divine.* All experience concurs in the testimony of revelation, that he is "the Lord God, merciful and gracious, long-suffering, and abundant in goodness and truth, keeping mercy for thousands, forgiving iniquity, and transgression, and sin." Exod. 34 : 6, 7.

If, then, there be any force in the divine example—if God be the pattern of his children, and it be our duty to resemble him—and if there be any virtue, any happiness, any glory in being godlike, what a motive to the right way is here afforded! It is *the divine way;* and we appeal to all those who aim at any degree of conformity to their Maker, to imitate him in these respects. "Be ye therefore followers of God, as dear children."

We would draw another motive from *the divine example as displayed in the person of Christ.* This motive is made use of by our Lord himself. He says, "A new commandment I give unto you, That ye love one another; as I have loved you, that ye also love one another." John 13 : 34. Paul exhorts, "Even as Christ forgave you, so also do ye." Colos. 3 : 13.

"Walk in love, as Christ also hath loved us." Eph. 5 : 2. Another apostle says, "Christ also suffered for us, leaving us an example that ye should follow in his steps: who when he was reviled, reviled not again; when he suffered, he threatened not; but committed himself to him that judgeth righteously." 1 Pet. 2 : 21, 23.

The life of Christ was a practical fulfilment of his own precepts. He faithfully trod that path which he marked out for others, and consecrated every step with his own toils and sufferings, and finally with his blood. His whole recorded history is a proof of the practical purport of his teachings, and of their applicability to every-day life. His very entrance into the world under a human form was an act of love to enemies. All his toils and trials were undergone with a direct view to the procuring of blessings for those who hated him. His walk through life was a perpetual exhibition of long-suffering; for even when not assailed in person, he was, *as God*, constantly blasphemed and disobeyed. Besides, however, this general display of kind dispositions, the treatment to which he was subjected while on earth afforded many particular occasions for their exercise. "He was oppressed and he was afflicted, yet he opened not his mouth: he is brought as a lamb to the slaughter, and as a sheep before her shearers is dumb, so he opened not his mouth." Isa. 53:7. Patiently he submitted to every indignity that the furious rabble chose to heap upon him—offering no resistance to the cross, the thorns, the nails, the spear—praying at the last, "Father, forgive them," and then pouring out his life's blood for the sake of those who murdered him. Never was there so sublime a fulfilment of the precept, "Love your enemies, bless them that curse you, do good to them that hate you, and pray for them which despitefully use you and persecute you."

"He that saith he abideth in him, ought himself also so to walk, even as he walked." 1 John, 2:6. Let the view of his bright example impel every Christian to its imitation. With our eyes fixed upon our glorious pattern, so lovely in his meek endurance, let us "*consider* him that endured such contradiction of sinners against himself, lest we be wearied and faint in our minds." Heb. 12:3. Did He who might have called down fire from heaven to consume his persecutors, choose rather to weep, and pray, and bleed for them? So, when the blood boils under an aggravated insult or injury, and the harsh reply hovers upon the lip, let the thought of Jesus change the bitter murmur into a forgiving prayer. Let us press forward in his sacred footsteps, rejoicing that our path to glory is so much like his. So doing, we shall not grope in the dark, for his every step has left its impression, distinct and ineffaceable; and the clear strong light of inspiration shines always upon them, and in revealing his pathway is "a lamp to our feet, and a light to our path." It is the height of the believer's aspirations, and will be the consummation of his glory, to be "*like him.*" Let us, by the cultivation of those affections and dispositions which he manifested, "walk even as he walked;" and at length, our hearts rid of all anger, malice, and resentment, and glowing with ardent, universal love to God and man, "*when he shall appear we shall be like him,* for we shall see him as he is."

VI. The strongest motive of all to the practice of the right way, is the fact that *God has commanded it.*

The precepts before us form a prominent part of God's revealed will. That will is the law of the universe, and the only correct rule of human duty. Its demands, whether admitted or denied by men—nay, even if opposed by a world in arms—God will in no instance repeal or modify. They come to us clothed with the sanction of the divine authority, and command our absolute, uncompromising obedience. Almighty power stands ready to enforce them, and the whole character of God assures us that he will not permit them to be violated with impunity. In dealing with our Maker, it is not our part to question, but implicitly to obey. It is a sufficient reason for these precepts, and for our obedience to them, that *God is their author.* When weighed against his command, every consideration of difficulty, danger, or irksomeness is of no account whatever. A simple "thus saith the Lord" answers every objection, solves every mystery, and leaves us nothing to do but to hear and obey.

The duty of love, when viewed in its largest sense, comprehends the whole of the divine law. "Love is the fulfilling of the law." Rom. 13:10. The various precepts growing out of it occupy, as we have seen, a very prominent place in the gospel, where their frequent and emphatic utterance characterizes them as important features of the Christian religion. Like bright, golden threads, they are inwrought with the whole system of revealed truth, and we cannot remove them from it without marring almost every page. They force themselves upon the attention of even the most careless reader of the Bible, and arrest our gaze far more frequently than many other truths to which the church has assigned a more prominent place in its creeds and practice. They are uttered, too, in language which we cannot misunderstand, and clothed with an authority which we must not disregard. And they have lost none of their binding power in the lapse of centuries. Though so much neglected, and by many despised, they yet stand forth to the eye of every Bible reader, their penalties unrevoked, a silent but powerful reproof to all who disobey them. Thus they shall stand for ever, occupying a place in the system of religion from which they cannot be wrested, and however overlooked or kept in the background, addressing men as authoritatively as any other of God's commands.

Need we say more to commend them to *the Christian?* What higher motive to their practice can be desired? Even were our obedience to them encompassed with tenfold greater difficulties; nay, were it to subject us to death itself, the fact that *God commands it* should outweigh all other considerations, and impel us to that obedience. We therefore urge this as of itself a sufficient motive. If we have presented others, it is not because we thought them necessary, but because they might influence some minds which do not sufficiently recognize the divine authority. The true disciple should require no other incentive to duty than the revealed will of God. This incentive we unquestionably have with regard to the duties of the *Right Way.*

CHAPTER VI.

APPLICATION OF THE RIGHT WAY.

It has been the misfortune of many, that while accepting these precepts as divine, they have at the same time regarded them rather as general expressions of duty than as specific commands. For this reason they have failed to apply them to all the ordinary circumstances and connections of social life. Yet they were formed with reference to them all, and are designed to be our guide in every relation of man to man. We shall now exhibit the mode of applying them to the intercourse of *individuals*, in the family, the neighborhood, and the church. The mode of their application to the intercourse of *nations*, will be considered in the second part of this work.

I. The family. If there be any bond in life which ought to be sacredly guarded from every thing that can put it in peril, it is that which unites the members of a family. If there be a spot upon earth from which discord and strife should be banished, it is the fireside.

There centre the fondest hopes and the most tender affections. It is the heart's *lower home*, where, more than in any other place, it is to be fitted for the upper mansions of our Father's house. Of all the different kinds of human intercourse, none is capable of conferring so much enjoyment when rightly improved, nor can any be made so great a source of wretchedness when perverted. Its members being thrown into perpetual contact, and to a great degree mutually dependent, it is in the power of each to promote or destroy the peace of all the others. For this and other reasons which will readily suggest themselves, there is no relation in life which so imperatively demands the practice of the right way.

1. It is of the first importance that the gospel method regulate the intercourse of *husband and wife*. How often is this most hallowed and endearing of human relationships imbittered by the practice of the wrong way on the part of one or both of them. A slight misunderstanding is perhaps allowed to go unexplained, or an offence unforgiven. Then affections are estranged, doubts and suspicions excited, peace banished from the once happy home, and two

hearts weighed down under a life-long grief. A single word of pardon, or a meek submission to injury, or a "soft answer," or a prayer, might in the first instance have prevented this wide breach. But by some strange infatuation, the cloud that was "no bigger than a man's hand" is permitted to grow until it blackens the whole horizon of their lives, and beats in pelting storms upon their heads. The result of such a course is often seen in the doom of the wretched inebriate, who seeks to drown his trials in his cups, and to find in the vicious and profligate that sympathy which his home has ceased to afford him. Often too it pales the cheek and wastes the life of her whom the husband had sworn to cherish, and whose outraged nature sinks under the wreck of its fond affections.

Let the law of love be made the absolute, inviolable law of home, and the trusty guardian of its joys. By a uniform mildness of temper and demeanor; by an habitual forbearance and conciliation; by a constant readiness to yield, forgive, or patiently endure; by a studied avoidance of all cause for provocation, whether great or small, upon either side; by maintaining a scrupulous watch upon both heart and tongue; by instantly banishing every beginning of strife, as they would a viper, from their bosoms; in short, by the cultivation, at any cost, of sweet, amiable dispositions, let both husband and wife promote their mutual harmony, and cement the bonds which unite them. "Wives, submit yourselves unto your own husbands, as it is fit in the Lord," Col. 3:18; "whose adorning, let it not be that outward adorning of plaiting of the hair, and of wearing of gold, or of putting on of apparel; but let it be the hidden man of the heart, in that which is not corruptible, even the ornament of a meek and quiet spirit, which is in the sight of God of great price." 1 Peter 3:3, 4. "Husbands, love your wives, even as Christ also loved the church, and gave himself for it." Eph. 5:25. "Husbands, love your wives, and be not bitter against them." Col. 3:19.

2. The precepts of the gospel should also govern the intercourse of *parents and children.* Suppose a child has disobeyed or otherwise injured his parent. Which course of conduct will best influence him to repentance and obedience—a passionate, threatening demeanor, or

one of love and kindness? Both observation and experience show that while the one course would only exasperate the little culprit, and render him sullen and hateful, the other would in most instances subdue his rebellious feelings, and restore him to a spirit of filial affection. We are not now speaking of the propriety of chastisement—this is by no means inconsistent with a loving and forgiving conduct. But the parent should see to it that neither his rebuke nor his punishment displays any spirit of resentment. There are occasions when the language of Socrates to his offending servant might well fill the lips of parents, "I would whip thee, *but that I am angry.*" The child's quick ear can readily detect the tone and manner of revenge, and he will not be slow to imitate it. He can also soon discover the accent of tender, yet sorrowing love, which in forgiving most clearly shows how it has been aggrieved; and his heart will penitently respond to it, and bow, melted, under its influence. No circumstances can justify *retaliatory* conduct towards a child. Those who would not rashly trample upon every fine affection of its budding nature, will be careful to avoid every thing approaching to it, either in word or action. "Fathers, provoke not your children to anger, lest they be discouraged." Col. 3:21.

3. These principles are equally applicable to the intercourse of *the younger members of the family*. In those petty strifes which so often mark their youthful sports, there are frequent occasions for exercising the spirit required of us. Indeed, they who are taught to improve all such opportunities will have acquired in early life habits of forbearance and self-control which will attend them in after-years, and prove to them a powerful safeguard.

We would therefore urge upon the youthful reader the importance of practising the right way. The young sometimes think it manly to be resentful and passionate, and to carry themselves in a blustering, threatening manner towards all who displease them. Such conduct is not manly, but brutish; and is it not better, nobler, happier, to be like God and Christ and angels, than like snarling brutes? As none are too young to offend, so none are too young to forgive. It is in the power of every youth or child to fulfil the duties which form the subject of this volume. Let such try to obey the gospel rules, and begin early to walk in these ways of "pleasantness" and paths of "peace." When any thing is done by another to vex or irritate you, think, "here is an opportunity to imitate God and Christ," and then answer it with kind words, and try to love, forgive, and bless your enemy. In all your sports or labors, at home, at school, or by the way; whether with parents, brothers and sisters, or playmates, seek to give offence to none, and if injured to show that you are above resenting it. Resolve that whatever others may do, you will do *right*. Thus obey God, and make yourselves and all about you happy.

Look at the family in which the gospel precepts are disregarded. It is a scene of constant turmoil. If one of its members chances to offend another, angry feelings are at once aroused, abusive words quickly follow, and perhaps they come to blows. Both are made ashamed and unhappy by yielding to the enemy that is in their own bosoms. Discords are perpetually occurring; the din of noisy strife prevails; and they who should be all loving and forbearing are, instead of it, envious and spiteful. Peace is almost a stranger there, while evil passions make it their home, and the demon of strife reigns triumphantly. How lovely, on the other hand, the spectacle presented by that family which is governed by the right spirit. Each strives to avoid giving offence, and is studiously considerate of the others' happiness. If, in an unguarded moment, one injures another, it is but the work of an instant to ask and receive forgiveness. Sweet, loving dispositions are cultivated by all, and each tries to surpass the other in his efforts for the common harmony. Smiles of affection and delight beam upon every face; each voice is schooled to tones of kindness; each heart glows with love; and the benediction of heavenly *peace* seems to abide upon that dwelling with such power that no black fiend of passion dare rear his head within it. It is like a concord of sweetest music, without one jarring note to mar its perfect harmony. It is like heaven, where the angels of God delight in the eternal flow of mutual affection, and are happy in for ever loving God and one another.

Who would not realize this lovely picture? It *may* be realized by all who will employ the appointed means. Let the precepts of the gospel be applied as they are designed to be; let them be inculcated upon every member of the family and enforced by a winning example; and they will be found to shed a holy charm upon the home which they govern, and to make the family circle what God designed that it should be, the most heaven-like scene upon earth.

II. Looking now at a wider sphere of human intercourse, let us consider the application of these principles to THE NEIGHBORHOOD.

The natural tastes and instincts of men impel them to group together, and dwell near each other. A peculiar relationship grows up between the families thus connected, which, like every other human tie, involves mutual interests, imposes mutual obligations, and is a powerful instrument of mutual happiness or misery. To which of these it ministers depends upon the principles that govern it. All are familiar with the meaning of the common expressions, "a good neighbor," and "a bad neighbor;" and all know what is that kind of conduct which renders a man the one or the other. It is generally the case that the passionate, resentful man is a curse to all who are about him; while he who is kind and forbearing, is esteemed a blessing to the community.

It is to be expected that the interests of neighbors will sometimes clash, and that selfishness, envy, or scandal will occasionally foment dissensions between them. What course is to be pursued under such circumstances? Suppose one neighbor has encroached upon the rights of another; shall the injured one avenge himself by a similar encroachment? He will only thereby plunge into yet deeper difficulties, and subject himself to a repetition of the offence. His act of retaliation will be likely to recoil upon himself. Or shall he resort to the arm of the law, and bring its weight to bear upon the offender? In aggravated cases, and when rendered necessary in order to protection or redress, this is a justifiable method; but when resorted to as a means of revenge, and for the gratification of malignant feelings, it is unquestionably the *wrong way*. The gospel method is the only one which can be adopted with advantage to either party. In demanding that the aggression be not resented, it discloses the means best calculated to allay strife, and secure the ends of truth and right. The neighbor who obeys its precepts will "resist not evil," but "overcome evil with good." If injured, he will frankly state his grievances to the offender, as soon as he can do so with no feeling or tone of bitterness, and courteously ask redress. Yet he will be careful to assure him that he cherishes no ill-will, and is ready to forgive and forget the past, and still to extend to him the hand of cordial friendship. Especially will he watch for an opportunity to prove his kind feelings by rendering him "good for evil." So doing, he will promote his own interests, and those of his neighbor and of the community, and bind the offender to himself in friendship more firm than ever.

A horse belonging to a pious man having once strayed into the road, a neighbor sent him to the pound. Meeting the owner soon afterwards, he told him what he had done, and added, "If I catch him in the road again, I 'll do it again." "Neighbor," said the other, "not long since I looked out of my window in the night, and saw your cattle in my meadow, and I drove them out and shut them in your yard; and *I 'll do it again.*" Struck with the reply, the man liberated the horse, paid the charges himself, and to this Christian at least, was ever after a "good neighbor." In how many instances is a course quite contrary to this pursued. An accidental breaking down of a fence, or straying of cattle, or a slight difference in regard to boundaries, or some petty trespass, over which neither, perhaps, had any control, has sometimes involved two parties in a tedious and expensive litigation from whose effects they never recovered; yet which might all have been avoided by the exercise of a little forbearance upon either side. Whole communities have been thus kept for years in a ferment by the ungovernable passions of one or two of their members. Were any neighborhood to be made up entirely of such persons, it would be little else than a pandemonium, an abode of all evil spirits, who would keep society in a state of perpetual discord. On the other hand, were there one whose members were all loving, forgiving, and forbearing, "in honor preferring one another," and mutually solicitous of the common good and the preservation of peace, it would indeed be a favored spot. Kind deeds and warm, generous sympathies would flow from hand to hand and from heart to heart, and the only strife would be as to which could best promote the happiness of all. Such a neighborhood would be comparatively free from those petty contentions which are now the bane of so many, would invite prosperity, and would secure to its members many invaluable blessings.

III. These precepts are designed for an especial application to THE CHURCH OF GOD, or to *the intercourse of Christians with one another.*

"A new commandment I give unto you, that ye love one another; as I have loved you, that ye also love one another. By this shall all men know that ye are my disciples, if ye have love one to another." John 13:34, 35. "Be kindly affectioned one to another with brotherly love; in honor preferring one another." Rom. 12:10. "See that ye love one another with a pure heart fervently." 1 Pet. 1:22. "Above all things have fervent charity among yourselves; for charity shall cover the multitude of sins." 1 Pet. 4:8. "We know that we have passed from death unto life, because we love the brethren. He that loveth not his brother abideth in death. Whosoever hateth his brother is a murderer: and ye know that no murderer hath

eternal life abiding in him." 1 John 3:14, 15.

We commend these passages to the earnest consideration of the Christian reader. The precept "*love one another*" comes to us from one who has an undoubted right to impose it, and with all the authority of "a new commandment." All must acknowledge its justness, and its binding force as a divine obligation. The gospel, however, not only insists upon love as a duty, but urges it as a necessary *fruit and evidence of piety*, for the satisfaction both of ourselves and others. Christ says, "By this shall all men know that ye are my disciples;" and an apostle assures us, "We know that we have passed from death unto life, because we love the brethren." The thought is a startling one, and full of suggestion to the pious mind. Let all who profess or believe themselves to have "passed from death unto life" ponder well these words, "He that loveth not his brother abideth in death." 1 John 3:14. See also 1 John 2:9, 10, 11; 3:10; 4:20.

But do professed Christians need these exhortations? Do not the children of God, the members of the household of faith, and the

travellers to a common heavenly home "love one another?" Alas, there are too many of them who might well exclaim, in the words of a saint of former times, "Blessed Jesus, *either these are not thy precepts, or we are not Christians.*" It is enough to sadden the hearts of all who love the cause of Christ, to see the church which he has redeemed with his precious blood so torn with intestine divisions. How often are its different branches arrayed in hostility upon slight points of controversy, foolishly expending upon one another those energies which should be concentrated against the common foe! What bitterness of feeling, what opprobriousness of epithet, what jealousy, envy, and malice have characterized much of the religious discussion of the church, causing a wide gulf of separation between those who should be joined in holiest sympathies! And if we look at individual churches, how many lie torn and bleeding under the sad effects of personal disputes. By an unbridled tongue, or mistaken zeal, or wicked envy and desire for precedence, our Saviour has often been "wounded in the house of his friends;" his cause has suffered, piety has declined, and obstacles almost insurmountable have been placed between the sinner and his salvation. Many a church has thus verified in its own unhappy experience those words of James, "Where envying and strife is, there is confusion and every evil work." Jas. 3:16. Eternity alone can reveal the amount of injury that has been done to the cause of Christ by the absence of brotherly love.

It was the highest encomium pronounced upon the early disciples, "See how these Christians love one another." But we afterwards find Paul severely rebuking some of them, styling them "carnal," and "babes in Christ;" "for whereas there is among you envying, and strife, and divisions, are ye not carnal, and walk as men?" 1 Cor. 3:3. Of course the guilty ones call these strifes by quite a different name. Those who are active in church dissensions style their conduct "a vindication of the truth," or "a manly independence," or "a holy indignation against the erring," or "a rectifying of abuses;" but it is a peculiarity of the gospel that it calls things by their right names, and there are few instances in which the more appropriate term would not be *carnal-mindedness*. Now when we remember that "to be carnally minded is death," how sad a scene is presented by those churches in which strifes and envyings exist! Under these forms carnality has invaded the very sanctuary of God, and is there sowing the seeds of a terrible death among the professed heirs of the heavenly life. As the opposite of this carnal spirit, the word inculcates the exercise of a loving and Christ-like disposition towards the erring. It stops not, however, with this, but clearly points out the line of conduct to be pursued towards a trespassing brother. "If thy brother shall trespass against thee, go and tell him his fault between thee and him alone: if he shall hear thee, thou hast gained thy brother. But if he will not hear thee, then take with thee one or two more, that in the mouth of two or three witnesses every word may be established. And if he shall neglect to hear them, tell it unto the church; but if he neglect to hear the church, let him be unto thee as a heathen man and a publican." Matt. 18:15–17.

1. The first step prescribed is a plain, frank statement to the offender of his fault. The parties at variance must meet face to face, that an opportunity may be afforded for mutual ex-

planations, or for a kind appeal or rebuke to the guilty one. Such a meeting would in many instances stop the beginnings of dissension; for it is often the case that one who has erred is longing for just such an opportunity to acknowledge and, if possible, repair his error.

2. This step, however, may sometimes be unsuccessful. It is then made our duty to resort to the second one, namely, a repetition of the interview in the presence of two or three witnesses, "that every word may be established." This injunction requires that those who assist in the effort be not merely witnesses to testify upon the subject before the church, if it should become necessary, but that they add the weight of their influence and kind Christian admonition. They should therefore be men of deep piety and sound judgment—"wise men," who are "able to judge between the brethren." Such will often effect, by their superior wisdom and discretion, that which others fail to accomplish.

3. "If he shall neglect to hear them," says Christ, "tell it unto the church." The grievance must, as a last resort, be laid before the

church, or its judicatory, which shall add its voice of mild yet firm authority, and enjoin repentance and reparation for the fault.

4. If, however, this step proves also ineffectual, and the offender remains insensible to every appeal of Christian love; "if he neglect to hear the church, let him be unto thee as a heathen man and a publican." The heathen and publicans were those with whom the Jews held no *religious* intercourse. Our Lord here requires that such as obstinately offend, and persist in wronging a fellow-Christian, be subjected to the discipline of the church. This should never be resorted to except when the previous steps have been faithfully employed; and then it should be done with all love and kindness, that the erring may if possible be still won, yet with firmness, that the peace and purity of the church may be maintained.

Throughout all these steps there is to be observed the same degree of tender forbearance and long-suffering. When thus conducted, there is reason to believe that they will be crowned with success, and go far towards maintaining that "fervent charity" which is "the bond of perfectness," the glory of the redeemed, and the heaven-born principle of the believer's present and future life.

The general spirit of these requirements, and indeed of the whole gospel, stands opposed to a mode of redress which is too common among professed Christians as well as others—*litigation*. This is pointedly rebuked by Paul as follows: "Dare any of you, having a matter against another, go to law before the unjust, and not before the saints? I speak to your shame. Is it so, that there is not a wise man among you? No, not one that shall be able to judge between his brethren? Now therefore there is utterly a fault among you, because ye go to law one with another. Why do ye not rather take wrong? why do ye not rather suffer yourselves to be defrauded?" 1 Cor. 6:1, 5–7. In these words the apostle finally solves a point which is sometimes disputed, and teaches us that we had better even suffer ourselves to be defrauded than exhibit to the world a spirit of contention. Of course there are occasions when justice requires that the person injuring us be punished with the rigors of the law, and when the cause of Christ would be more prejudiced by a quiet submission than by an obtaining of legal redress. Such instances, however, are comparatively rare, there being few differences among Christians which may not be more happily adjusted by their reference to some "wise man" who is "able to judge between his brethren," or which, if not thus settled, had not better be meekly endured than *legally* revenged.

Our present codes of civil law are such as every citizen may justly be proud of. Founded, as the wisest legislators admit, upon the precepts of the gospel, they go far towards securing the end of those precepts, the practice of the *right way*. Yet is it not too often the case that the privileges afforded by them are abused, and made a means of retaliation and revenge? A suit at law is often prompted by those angry feelings which, in a state of less refinement and civilization, would exhibit itself in open blows. It is often the disguised expression of that hatred to one's brother which, however manifested, constitutes a murder. And even when entered upon with calmness and brotherly affection, how often does the progress of the trial excite bitter feelings upon both sides, and display to the world a spirit that is far from Christ-like!

We would by no means undervalue the laws of the state—they are essential to its well-being; but let them not be perverted from their high office as the defence of justice and shield of the oppressed, to the ignoble one of a means of revenge. At all events, let those who follow the meek and lowly Jesus be governed, as they profess to be, by that source of all law and equity, the word of God, and accept as their rule of life that code whose demands are all summed up in the one word, *love.*

Such is the mode prescribed in the gospel for regulating the intercourse of the brethren. How beautifully does it contrast, in its divine nature and happy tendencies, with the way that is too frequently practised among them! Were it more generally observed, the church would not exhibit to the world such gross inconsistencies as now characterize her, nor be taunted with being false to her acknowledged principles. She would no longer present the spectacle of a torn and bleeding body, wounded, not by her enemies, but by her avowed friends and members. Then the proverb would once more be, "See how these Christians love one another." Beautiful would be the appearance she would then present, keeping "the unity of the spirit in the bonds of peace." Then Christianity would be seen and confessed a divine institution, and its very loveliness, as made known in the lives of its adherents, would win many to its standard. Then too, not only causes of offence and stumbling would be removed, but instead of them would be the more active labors of God's united people; churches whose dissensions now grieve the Spirit, would be visited by his influences; the word would have new power, and united, sympathizing prayer be attended with new efficacy; religion would be revived, saints edified, sinners saved, and God glorified.

We therefore appeal to all who love our Lord Jesus Christ, to "follow after the things which make for peace." Your own life and happiness demand it, for "he that hateth his brother is a murderer, and ye know that no murderer hath eternal life abiding in him." The interests of the church demand it; for how can she hope or pray for success while distracted by civil feuds and divisions? The honor of the meek and lowly Jesus demands it, for his name and cause are too often disgraced by the unworthy strifes of his avowed disciples. The welfare of the world demands it, for the reign of peace will never prevail, except it begin with the church. It is not enough that we pray and labor for that glorious consummation; we must second our labors, and prove the sincerity of our prayers, by ourselves practising that right way which we commend to others, just as Jesus enforced by the power of his own example every truth which he uttered with his lips. The interests of immortal souls demand it, for weak minds are stumbling to perdition over the faults of Christians. Many reject that religion whose precepts are so plainly violated by its professors; and it is to be feared, that with some the angry word or bitter retort uttered by a disciple, may be the turning-point which seals their endless destiny. As then, Christian, you value your own soul, and the souls of your brethren—as you value the cause of Christ, the interests of the world, and the salvation of those about you—as you would not weaken and distract the power which, under God, is to convert the nations—as you would be free from the blood of souls, "*follow after the things which make for peace.*" "*Be of one mind, live in peace, and the God of love and peace shall be with you.*"

PART II.

THE GOSPEL APPLIED TO THE INTERCOURSE OF NATIONS.

CHAPTER VII.

NATIONAL INTERCOURSE—THE GOSPEL APPLICABLE TO IT.

BOTH nations and individuals are governed by the same natural laws. The same instincts, necessities, and dependencies attend both, and alike impel them to hold intercourse with one another. God has so framed our globe, with its different climates and various products, that every nation, while containing within itself all the necessaries of life, is compelled to look to almost all the other nations for many of its comforts and luxuries. As the result of this, we find them engaged in commerce, or the profitable exchange of their products and manufactures. This brings the subjects of different governments into friendly contact, and establishes an identity of interest between them. With the advance of civilization, the tribes and kingdoms have more and more felt the necessity of this intercourse, until now, one wall of exclusive policy after another having been broken down, the nations are rapidly commingling. Men are beginning to feel that they are all members of one common family, and the different countries are fast becoming, in point of fact, a neighborhood.

The *necessity* of this intercourse has become too well established to require any argument. The nations, by an irresistible impulse, *will associate* together; and it is considered as unwise and as unnatural for one of them to sever its connections with the others, as it is for an individual to withdraw entirely from the society of his fellows.

It is equally evident to the observing mind that this intercourse is *designed for the good of men*. Experience proves that in proportion as it is amicably maintained, our social happiness is directly augmented. It in a measure extends to every nation the literature, science, arts, and manufactures of every other. As in a community much is gained to every member by the division of labor, the rivalry of skill, and the relations of each to the others, so it is with nations. In both instances, also, kind affections and sympathies are called into exercise, and made a powerful source of happiness. Especially it is true of them both, that they can greatly promote one another's spiritual well-being. The bearings of national intercourse upon the dissemination of Bible truth, and the multiplied instrumentalities for the world's conversion, are plain to every beholder. Yet, as in the one case, so in the other, it can be made a powerful instrument of evil. If abused, it may become a curse, whose magnitude is proportioned to the vastness of the interests which it involves. In the one instance the effects of contention are generally limited to a very few persons—to two or three disputants, or at most to a family or neighborhood; in the other they extend to millions. If, then, it be important that the intercourse of man with man be governed by right principles, it is of far greater importance that that of nation with nation be so governed. Every reason which applies to the one is applicable with accumulated force to the other.

Alas, that in this respect also we must behold the sad perversion of God's providential arrangements for our good. Those wrong principles which so much imbitter the private and social relations of men, govern to a yet greater degree the relations of the masses. The same foul passions which, in the infancy of our race, produced a murderer, have, from the very infancy of tribes and kingdoms, filled the earth with wholesale violence and slaughter. If we attentively consider the intercourse of nations, we behold a state of things that is most repulsive and soul-sickening. We see kingdom rising up against kingdom in deadly conflict. We see great masses of human beings arrayed against each other for avowed purposes of destruction, and thousands upon thousands of them cut down—costly sacrifices to vengeance or ambition. We see *men*, possessed of immortal souls, and ennobled with godlike capacities, pressing on in herds to a worse than brutal slaughter; and then left wallowing in their blood, while new victims take their places and share their fate. Man prostitutes his noble powers to the most ignoble ends. Minds whose skill and wisdom might have blessed the world, and enhanced our social comforts, expend their energies in devising modes and instruments of warfare, and plotting death to thousands. Hands that might have been powerful to help and encourage, are devoted to mutual slaughter. Voices that might have been eloquent to cheer and animate to duty, are mistuned to heaven-offending blasphemies, and curses on their fellows. Manly strength, which if rightly directed might have increased the sum of human happiness, assumes the form of wild, brute violence. Instead of the honorable rivalry of love and duty, is seen the disgraceful competition of desolation, rapine, and murder.

Scarcely has there been a period in the history of our earth, when the above dark picture would not apply to some portions of it. There have indeed been intervals of peace, but generally so brief that they appeared to be only breathing spells or truces, in which the combatants rested upon their arms, and gained strength for more violent onsets. Strife seems to have been the element of almost all national existence. Nearly every throne has been, to a greater or less degree, propped up by the slain bodies of both its subjects and its enemies.

If we look for the *cause* of this wide-spread calamity, we shall find it to be the same that lies at the root of all individual contention, namely, a resort to the *wrong way* of conducting intercourse and adjusting differences. We behold both the reason of this curse and wherein lies its remedy, in the fact that it is a violation of the precepts of the gospel. This we shall hereafter show. Perhaps, however, it is necessary at this stage of our discussion to prove that *those precepts are applicable to nations equally with individuals.*

While the gospel has been, for centuries, gradually conforming the spirit and conduct of *individuals* to itself, it has thus far been lamentably disregarded by *governments*. Even in those countries which are professedly Christian, and where the law of God is recognized as the law of the land and the foundation of its jurisprudence, it has been studiously excluded from the national councils. As a necessary consequence of these mistaken views, the progress of nations, *as such*, has been much slower than that of the individuals of whom they are composed; and the anomaly is this day presented of their retaining and practising a custom which they have long since abolished among their subjects as barbarous and unjust. While the gospel has been allowed to mould the *civil* law until it has brought it to its present stage of perfection, it has not been permitted, by any means to the same degree, to govern the *law of nations.* The singular spectacle is therefore presented of two different and widely opposite rules of right controlling the internal and external affairs of every country; and men are required to act in their collective capacity precisely contrary to the course which is required of them as individuals. The inconsistency of this state of things is manifest, and should lead us to suspect that one or the other of these two rules is wrong. Which of them is so, it requires no effort to determine. The only rule of right, the revealed will of God, is as applicable to nations as it is to individuals.

All the acknowledged authorities upon international law agree in affirming that a nation is to be regarded *as a moral person.* Vattel says, "Nations are under the same obligations that are binding upon men in their intercourse one with another." Chancellor Kent says, "They are properly regarded as moral persons." This view is a just one, and is founded upon the fact that the nation is a collection of individuals, and that the government is their representative. It naturally follows from this that the same general laws which govern each one separately, ought to govern them all united; that men possess in their collective capacity the same rights, the same duties, and the same accountability to God which they have as individuals; and that their rulers or representatives are under those moral obligations which bind the people for whom they act. If, therefore, the gospel addresses its precepts to *men*, it is equally binding upon them whether they act together as masses, or separately as individuals. If the gospel imposes its obligations upon *every moral person*, then those obligations bind with full force the nation, which competent authorities have said should be considered and treated as a "moral person."

It is, from the very nature of the case, impossible that there be *two opposite rules of right*. If there are two which conflict together, no other evidence is needed that one of them is erroneous. Right exists in itself, and is not created by circumstances. If any deed is wrong, or forbidden by God's law, no combination of circumstances can make it otherwise. Every thing which it is right or wrong for one or two persons to do, is the same for a hundred or a thousand. If any one questions this, let him attempt to assign the limit where one obligation ceases and an opposite one takes its place. Is it when ten persons are acting together, or fifty, or five hundred? Can men, by thus banding, sin with impunity, and violate every gospel precept without incurring guilt? If this were so, would not the gospel rule be sadly defective? But it is not so; and the world has suffered much because men have not seen the full perfection of the law of God. The fault lies not in the gospel, but in those who have presumed to limit its application. The very fact that the duties of Christianity are binding upon each person, proves them to be binding upon all. Men cannot divest themselves of their individual accountability. After all the efforts that are commonly made to that end, the soldier cannot be converted into a mere machine, nor shift the whole responsibility of his conduct upon the master-spirit who claims the sole right to animate him. At the bar of God he will be judged as an individual, and his own guilt cannot be extinguished in the plea that he committed crime at the bidding of another. It is the duty of every individual in the nation to obey the gospel. If all were to do so, how could they unitedly disobey it?

That there must be some rule of right to govern the intercourse of nations, is generally admitted. The fact of the existence of a code of international law shows the felt necessity for such a rule. Where, then, shall it be found? There is but one source of human law, the revealed will of God. To it we are indebted for the greater part of our civil codes—the most eminent jurists having acknowledged that they are founded upon the Bible. That Bible is not so imperfect as to have limited its precepts to certain relations and circumstances of life, leaving others unprovided for. We know that it is complete, because God is its author, and that therefore it must be designed for application to nations as well as individuals. To it we are to look for the rule of national intercourse. If it contained laws relating especially to governments, it would be our duty to adopt them. As, however, it does not contain them, we can only conclude that its wise Author, who knows precisely what our circumstances require, *intended that the same rule should apply in general to both individuals and nations.* "The *rule of right* which binds the single individual, binds two or three when gathered together—binds conventions and congregations of men—binds villages, towns, and cities—binds states, nations, and empires—clasps the whole human family in its seven-fold embrace."

This rule of right is contained in the gospel; and it is only by obedience to it that nations can attain to the *Right Way* of conducting intercourse.

CHAPTER VIII.

THE EVILS OF WAR.

BEFORE proceeding to a special application of the gospel to this branch of our subject, let us take a rapid survey of *the evils of war.*

If the picture of individual discords is a sad one, that of national strife is still more so. Our theme rises in melancholy interest, as we are now called to contemplate this very darkest side of depraved humanity. The view is a soul-sickening one, and well calculated to overwhelm the mind with disgust and horror. Its details, if truthfully depicted, would be enough to stir up every fountain of mournful emotion; and he is indeed to be pitied who can dwell upon them without tender sympathy and grief. But let us not therefore shrink from them. It is to be feared that an undue sensibility upon this subject has caused the Christian world to forget its duty, and prevented it from putting forth those efforts which might, long before this, have abolished the terrible curse. We have been like the sick man, who, while painfully conscious of disease, should refuse to look upon his wounds and putrefying sores, lest he be shocked by the view of their corruption. How much better to know the worst, that he might be led to employ the means of cure. And how much better it would be for mankind if they would seriously consider this their deep-seated leprosy, and in full view of its dangerous character, earnestly and patiently apply to it the divine remedy!

I. Glancing first at some of its lesser evils, consider ITS INCALCULABLE WASTE OF PROPERTY.

We say *incalculable*, for no arithmetic can compute the immense amount which has thus been sacrificed. In order to form any adequate conception of its cost to the world, we must be able to estimate not only the actual outlays incurred in every war, and which are met by public appropriations, but also the value of the fields laid waste, of the towns and cities destroyed, of the peaceful occupations abandoned, and of the labors of the soldiers, had they been engaged in tilling the soil, commerce, or manufactures. We must add the losses occasioned by the general derangement of business, more or less affecting every individual of the warring countries. To these must be added the vast amount of good which might have been accomplished had this wealth been expended in other channels, the physical sufferings it might have relieved, and the spiritual, soul-saving blessings it might have conferred upon millions who are destitute of them. Who can compute all these? What mind can adequately estimate the sum which such thoughts suggest? We are bewildered in the attempt to measure it, or to assign any limit to this fearful waste.

1. Look at some of the *direct expenses* of war. The last war of the United States with Great Britain cost our nation about fifty millions of dollars a year; and our war with Mexico was waged at an expense of more than one hundred millions. Our Revolutionary war cost England six hundred and eighty millions. According to official reports, the military and naval expenditures of the British government for the year ending March 31, 1855, amounted to £49,812,637, or about $249,063,185. England alone, in the wars occasioned by the French Revolution, spent more than five thousand millions; and it is estimated that she spent about ten thousand millions in "wars having for their

object, first the humiliation of the Bourbons, and then their restoration to the throne." As nearly as can be ascertained, the wars of Christendom during the twenty-two years from 1793 to the peace of 1815, were carried on at an expense of about *fifteen thousand millions of dollars!*

Perhaps we cannot better exhibit the immense burdens thus imposed upon the nations, than by glancing at some of those *debts* which have been contracted by all Europe in order to the prosecution of war. The public debt of Great Britain alone, in January, 1854, was £770,923,000, or about $3,854,615,000—all of which is the growth of wars undertaken since the year 1688. The interest upon this debt, and the cost of its management, amounts to nearly $150,000,000 every year. Well said Canning and Brougham, "England is under bonds of eight hundred million pounds sterling to keep the peace." And she is not alone. Every European nation is weighed down under the same mighty incubus, and its revenues absorbed and its inhabitants taxed to an oppressive degree by debts incurred in war. Without going into detail, it will suffice to say, that according to official estimates carefully collated and summed up, the entire war debt of Europe in 1840 was found to be not less than ten thousand million dollars, which is an average of fifty dollars to each of its inhabitants. This is supposed to be five times as much as all the coin in the world. The mere interest upon this sum, at six per cent., would be six hundred millions a year, or almost two millions every day!

And all this—*for what?* In most instances, to gratify ambition and the lust for fame and power; to avenge real or fancied insults; to trample upon the rights of the feeble; to achieve exploits which should put humanity to the blush; to plant national standards upon the reeking graves of subjects, and unfurl them to the air that is burdened with the frenzied groans and imprecations of the maimed and dying; to depopulate earth of much of its sinew and strength; to brutalize and then destroy millions of our fellow-men, and to people hell with murderers. *Two millions of dollars* devoted *every day* by Christian nations to such purposes as these! It is nearly three hundred times as much as is given by those nations for the spread of the gospel and the evangelization of man.

2. But we have only begun to contemplate this fearful waste. Let us look at some of those *incidental* losses which are inseparably connected with war in its crippling and destruction of a nation's private wealth. The exports and imports of the United States for 1855, amounted to about five hundred millions of dollars. It has been supposed that in the event of a war with a maritime power, one half of this would be liable to be seized by the enemy. What a blow to our prosperity would this be, especially as the amount thus lost would be added to the increased expenditures which would then be required of us. An eminent statesman once estimated the annual production of the United States at nearly ninety dollars to each inhabitant. Reckoning our present population at twenty-six millions, and supposing the loss of property by war to be one-fifth, our annual sacrifice would be nearly four hundred and sixty-eight millions of dollars.

The incidental losses of property by war cannot, however, be expressed by figures. Could we trace the course of almost any army, we should find it marked with the most destructive ravages. Like the plague of locusts, they desolate every fruitful field which lies in their path, and pillage and burn whole towns and cities. In the war with Russia, 1855, the allied fleets destroyed in a few days two hundred and forty-five Russian vessels, laden with provisions for the army in the Crimea. At Berdiansk and Chenitschesk more than seven million rations of corn, flour, and breadstuffs were destroyed, and at Kertch upwards of four and a half million pounds of corn and flour. The armies of Attila and the Huns, in the thirteenth century, so ruined a tract of many hundred miles from the Caspian to the Indus, that "five centuries have not been sufficient to repair the ravages of four years." Thirty thousand villages and hamlets are said to have been destroyed in the Thirty Years' war. A thousand of them a year! It is said that Napoleon's army, during a march of a hundred and fifty miles from Moscow, set fire to every house. Imagine, then, the desolations which have been thus wrought by all the millions of soldiers who have from time to time traversed the fairest portions of our globe, sweeping Sirocco-like over the gardens of the world, and blighting them into deserts!

Besides all this, war cripples private enterprise, causes capital to lie idle and unproductive, and paralyzes all the ordinary methods of acquiring wealth. The hum of business is silenced by the roar of artillery, and the peaceful sounds of the arts and manufactures are hushed to a dreary pause before the sharp notes of war. The farmer rests despondingly upon his idle plough, for there is no foreign market for his products; the mechanic sits listlessly in his shop, for there is no outlet for his workmanship; the merchant closes his counting room, or "suspends payment," for his ships are rotting at the wharves from very disuse; the poor day-laborer begs, or starves, or *fights* for bread, for most of the avenues of industry are closed, public improvements are suspended, and capital is withheld from use. Says a letter from St. Petersburgh, August, 1855, "The situation of Russia to-day may be summed up in two words—misery and general discontent. The war has struck a fatal blow to commerce, to production, and to industry. There has, in fact, been raised, by successive recruitments, more than a quarter of the able-bodied laborers, and it is impossible to find a sufficient number for tilling the ground, or for working in the factory." Thus all classes suffer to an incalculable degree under the pecuniary embarrassments of a state of war.

3. We should also include in this view the *direct expenditures occasioned by the war spirit in times of peace.* In the fiscal year ending June 30, 1855, the total expenses of the United States government amounted to about sixty-six millions of dollars. Of this, more than twenty-eight millions was appropriated for war purposes alone. From the beginning of our present form of government in 1789 to the year 1855, the appropriations for the military establishment were $563,532,482, and those for the naval establishment $280,640,779, making the total of $844,173,261. During the same period the civil expenses, exclusive of those on account of the public debt, reached only $366,109,657, or less than one half the above amount, although the whole period included but three years and a half of actual war. Deducting from the above naval and military appropriations the appropriations for war, we find that *nearly five hundred millions of dollars have been devoted to preparation for war in times of peace.* The tax upon

the English people, for the payment of interest on their war debt, and the support of the army, navy, etc., has been of late about two hundred millions per annum. At the same time twenty millions a year has met all the other expenses of the government; so that every British tax payer pays ten cents for past and anticipated wars to every cent appropriated for other purposes. If we suppose the standing armies of Europe, in time of peace, to be three million men, a close calculation will show that their aggregate cost to their governments cannot be less than $1,200,000,000 every year. To this add the immense cost of the American and European navies, and of the fortifications, arsenals, and other expensive means of attack and defence, and we have a sum expended for war purposes *wholly in times of peace* which is almost beyond computation.

In view of all this enormous waste, it has been asserted that the real cost of war is at least *four times as great as its direct expenditures.* If this be the case, we must estimate the wars of Europe for the twenty-two years preceding the peace of 1815, at *sixty thousand millions of dollars!* We have confined our view to these later wars, because there are reliable statistics with regard to them. If we could form any remote approximation to the amounts thus perverted during the last few centuries, the array of figures would be truly appalling. If we could embrace in our view all the pecuniary losses which men have *ever* thus sustained, it would be enough to stagger the strongest mind in the effort to conceive of it. That would then be esteemed a very low estimate, though a startling one, which supposes that "war has wasted at least fifty times as much as all the property now on the face of the globe!"

Now if war be wrong, we must regard a large part of this wealth as diverted from a right channel into a wrong one. In concluding this view, therefore, let us take into consideration the vast benefits which would result from the legitimate employment of the amounts thus worse than wasted. The labors of the American missionaries in the Sandwich Islands, for the period of about thirty years, cost the Christians of the United States $882,683, or less than the expense of *building one line-of-battle ship, and keeping it in service for one year!* As the result of that "thirty years' war" against idolatry, a degraded heathen nation has become Christianized, and is now sending forth its own missionaries to other and distant fields. The army and navy appropriations of the United States are about twenty-five millions of dollars a year. Who can estimate the good which might be accomplished, were this sum applied to purposes tending to elevate and Christianize, instead of degrading mankind? This money would give a free common-school education to all the five million children in our land. If we add to it the annual cost of our militia, there remains a sum sufficient to support every college, theological, medical, and law school in the United States, making them free to all, besides sustaining an army of colporteurs and ministers, who would reflect far greater honor upon us, and secure more prosperity to the nation, than can ever be derived from the most imposing army of brave soldiers. Were only a tithe of the sums annually sacrificed to the war spirit in Christian Europe in times of peace to be thus devoted, there would be enough to feed all the hungry, to clothe all the naked, to educate all the ignorant, to place the Bible in every destitute family, to flood the globe with religious books and tracts, and, by the blessing of God, to civilize and Christianize all the heathen upon the face of the earth. It would suffice to erect churches in every village and hamlet, and to support a million ministers of the word, whose voices should every Sabbath publish to the nations the glad tidings of peace. It would sustain and increase those instrumentalities by which God is converting the world to himself; would carry on the battle of the Lord, defeat the enemies of truth, and plant the gospel banner on every hill and in every valley of the habitable globe.

Christian, can you withhold your efforts from the work of destroying that enemy to God and man which is preventing such mighty and eternally blessed results? "*Shall the sword devour for ever?*"

II. Another of the evils of war, and one which is immeasurably more disastrous than its waste of property, is ITS MORAL EFFECTS, both upon those engaged in it, and upon the community at large.

Robert Hall has justly observed, "War reverses, with respect to its objects, all the principles of morality. It is nothing less than a temporary repeal of all the principles of virtue, and is a system from which almost all the virtues are excluded, and into which nearly all the vices are incorporated." Napoleon recognized the importance of a depraved character to a good soldier. He allowed no chaplain in his army, and was accustomed to say, "The worse the man, the better the soldier; and *if soldiers are not corrupt, they should be made so.*" Of a similar character is the testimony of the Duke of Wellington, who is reported to have said, "Men of nice scruples about religion have no business in the army or navy." War is the concentration of all iniquities. There is not one of the black catalogue of crimes which it does not foster, while those of the deepest dye are actually demanded by it. From its very nature it transforms large numbers of those engaging in it into thieves and murderers. It openly sets at defiance every law of God; subverts truth, love, justice, purity, and temperance; undermines the strongest virtues; obliterates, for the time, all that is lovely and amiable in human character; blunts the moral sense; drowns the voice of conscience and of God, and renders its votaries a prey to the worst of passions. It sows broadcast through the homes of Christendom seeds which grow up to a harvest of impiety, and which, but for the word of divine promise, we might well fear could never be eradicated. It assimilates men to demons, and under the specious disguises of patriotism, chivalry, and glory, opens the flood-gates of evil, and deluges the world with guilt.

1. Look at its *immoral effects upon soldiers.* It is a direct appeal to the most unworthy passions of their nature. It calls forth and exercises anger, jealousy, envy, hatred, and resentment. It nourishes malignant dispositions, and frowns severely upon every emotion of love or pity for "*the enemy.*" It requires and applauds that fiendish spirit which is essential to its wholesale murders; and he who is the most blinded by it, and the most recklessly wreaks his vindictive malice upon others, is styled a hero. A British officer who took part in the battle of Inkerman, says of the combatants in that engagement, "I saw them hanging on each other like gnashing bull-dogs, and roll on the ground over and over again, stabbing, tearing, cutting, and wrangling, *like men who had lost every characteristic of humanity, and acquired more*

than tiger ferocity." A soldier, who was engaged in one of the battles in the Crimea, says in a letter to his friends, "I never certainly felt less fear in my life than I did at that time; and I hope that God will forgive me, *for I felt more like a devil than a man!*" The very mainspring of a battle is, in most instances, *retaliation to the death;* and he whose bosom is not fired with the purpose of murderous revenge is branded with cowardice.

One of its worst evils is the *insensibility to human misery* which it engenders. It brutalizes men into an utter contempt for others' woes. It carries them to such a pitch of indifference, that they can behold unmoved the dying pangs of thousands. Nay more, the eyes that should be suffused with tears at the spectacle of the battle-field, learn to feast on it with joy; and the view of mangled limbs and heaped-up carcasses thrills the bosom of the "good soldier" with exquisite delight. He replies to the groans and shrieks of the dying with shouts of exultation, and cheers his comrades on over their prostrate bodies to the infliction of the same miseries upon others. Says Labaume, writing of the French war with Russia, "This campaign was the more frightful, as it demoralized our character, and gave birth to vices till then unknown to us; and they who had been generous, humane, and upright, became selfish, avaricious, and unjust." The same writer, after describing the horrors which attended the return of the French troops from Moscow, says, "These horrors, so far from exciting our sensibility, only hardened our hearts. Preserving the plunder of Moscow was preferred by most to the pleasure of saving a comrade. We heard around us the groans of the dying, and the plaintive voices of those who were abandoned; but all were deaf to their cries, and if any one approached them when on the point of death, it was for the purpose of stripping them, and searching whether they had any remains of food." The following extract from a private letter was extensively copied by the British press, with the heading, "A *brave* Guardsman's use of his Mother's Letters." "I don't want to see any more crying letters come to the Crimea from you. Those that I have received I *have put into my rifle* after loading it, and have fired them at the Russians, because you appear to have a strong dislike to them. If you had seen as many killed as I have, you would not have as many *weak ideas* as you have; besides being present when the shot, shell, and musketry were flying past and ringing around you, bursting and killing hundreds on your right hand and on your left, and yourself kept firing until the sweat streamed from you." To what a state of brutish degradation must they have become reduced, who can thus crush all the best instincts and sympathies of the human heart! Yet such is the inevitable tendency of war.

Look, too, at some of the *crimes and vices* which are inseparable from it, and in which the large majority of the soldiery engage. *War is robbery.* Alexander the Great once asked a pirate who had been brought before him, "By what right do you infest the seas?" He fearlessly replied, "By the same that you infest the universe. But because I do it in a small ship, I am called a robber; and because you do the same acts with a great fleet, you are called a conqueror." Of an equally truthful import was the language of the Scythian ambassadors to the same monarch: "You boast that the only design of your marches is to extirpate robbers. You yourself are the greatest robber in the world." What, we would ask, is the difference between the warrior and the highwayman? By what rule of equity can we distinguish between the crime of forcibly despoiling another's goods under the cover of darkness, and upon a lonely road, and despoiling them openly and by daylight? If the action of stealing be a crime, the fact that numbers are engaged in it cannot make it a virtue. Every principle of justice which applies to individuals, is applicable with a tenfold greater force to nations. If a single theft is wrong, how much worse is that which is perpetrated by a band of ten or twenty thousand robbers! Every difference between the highwayman and the soldier is in favor of the former; for he is perhaps tempted to his crime by want, while war robs from choice, and often for the sake of havoc. The one generally allows his victim to choose between surrendering his money or his life; the other more often couples its crime with that of murder. Besides, the immense thefts committed by a ravaging army in time of war are not the only ones to be attributed to it. Having become schooled to pillage, and unfitted for honorable labor, many of the soldiers afterwards become petty thieves or pirates. "War makes thieves," said Machiavelli, "and peace hangs them."

War is subversive of the Sabbath. It only recognizes this holy day by dissipation and revelry. Marches and even battles are then conducted with little or no hesitation. The battle of Waterloo was fought on the Sabbath—also that of Inkerman. In some parts of Europe it is the day set apart for militia musters and the parade of the regular army. In many places martial music salutes the ears of devout worshippers who "keep holy day," and the praises that go up to the Prince of peace are often drowned with the peculiar notes of war. Of course these parades attract large numbers of curious idlers, who do their part towards robbing God of the services appropriate to the day. A letter from the Crimea, Oct. 1854, says, "The Russians opened a very heavy cannonade on us this morning; *they have always done so on Sundays.* Divine service was performed with a continued bass of cannon rolling through the responses and liturgy."

War encourages intemperance. A secretary of war in the United States once observed, "It will never do to give up the use of ardent spirits in the army and navy, for *no one enlists when he is sober.*" If this be even an approximation to the truth—as probably there are very many exceptions to it—our army and navy must be mostly composed of persons addicted to this vice. Certain it is that the "grog ration" has been a fruitful source of evil to our marine. The militia system, also, has been a strong-hold of intemperance. Until quite recently, almost every muster-field has been surrounded with booths and stalls for the sale of intoxicating liquors. Many of the spectators as well as soldiers, who have there acquired a fondness for the cup, have afterwards become confirmed inebriates. There is, too, a kind of connection between war and wine. Each of them inflames the passions, and gives an appetite for the other. Indeed, it is sometimes deemed necessary for the soldier to madden and brutalize himself with drink before a battle, as the best preparation for it. A writer from "before Sebastopol," in 1855, says, "In one division which I know of, two hundred and ten gallons of rum are drank every day, *and it is all required.* The consumption of the whole army must be *about a thousand gallons daily.*" In one of the engagements in the Crimea, we are told, "The Russian soldiers were all 'as drunk as fiddlers,' and fought like madmen. About five hundred prisoners were taken, all almost too drunk to stand upright." We commend these facts to the attention of those who are so nobly and successfully battling with intemperance throughout the world, and ask whether the cause of peace and that of temperance should not go hand in hand?

War is a school of profanity. "He swears like a trooper" is a common mode of describing great profaneness. This vice is fashionable among soldiers, and is esteemed by some of them the badge of a gentleman. For an officer to give his orders without interlarding them with oaths, would be considered vulgar and unmanly. Indeed, so customary has it become, that the opinion has been gravely maintained that "the work of a ship cannot be done without swearing." The battle-field always resounds with blasphemies, and its air is filled with horrid oaths and imprecations.

War fosters licentiousness. Soldiers are for the most part dissolute men, and the means of gratifying their depraved lusts are seldom wanting. This vice, it is estimated, has swept away more of them than the sword. It has been remarked that the breaches of the seventh commandment in every nation are proportioned to its warlike spirit, or to the size of its army and navy. Decency forbids that we present details which might be given upon this subject. The evil is, however, well known and generally admitted.

War is murder. No species of plausible reasoning can prove it otherwise than a clear violation of the command, "Thou shalt not kill." The facts that it is deliberate, and sanctioned by custom and the authority of a sovereign or nation, so far from palliating its guilt, only increase it. Private murders, which so powerfully affect us, and the perpetrators of which we so bitterly denounce and hang, are far less to be execrated. They are generally committed in the violence of sudden passion. Wars are premeditated, and the result of calm debate and cool calculation. In the one case, a man kills his enemy; in the other, men are bid to kill those whom they have never before seen, and with whom they have had no personal differences. In the one, a single being is launched into eternity; in the other, thousands. War, too, inflicts deaths of extremest suffering. The greater number of its victims linger for hours, and many of them for days, in the most aggravated torture, and groan out their lives amid every thing that can make death ghastly and unwelcome, and thus go to the judgment of Him who has said, "No murderer hath eternal life abiding in him." Are those who voluntarily hurl them there any the less murderers because "obeying orders," and preferring to serve a brutal sovereign or cómmander rather than God? No; the brand of Cain is upon their brows, and although not seen by blind human justice, is plainly evident to the just Almighty.

2. Look at the *immoral effects of war upon communities.* We can imagine the influence which an army of criminals and vicious persons would exert upon the public at large. Their example must necessarily infect large numbers with whom they associate in times of peace. Especially do the public morals always suffer at the seat of war. Under the corrupting influences of an invading or defending army, the peaceful inhabitants become familiarized with

scenes of grossest iniquity. Their hearts become gradually hardened to the view of human suffering, and grow brutal and unfeeling. Malignant passions are aroused, and glow fiercely in many bosoms. The restraints of virtue, openly set at defiance by so many around them, lose much of their power. As the means of honorable subsistence diminish, the temptations to crime are increased, and the weak and irresolute yield to them as their only method of relief. Piety languishes; religion becomes a byword; profanity, intemperance, and profligacy reign triumphant; the solemn services of God's house are suspended, or at least neglected, and hell seems to hold high carnival. A deserter from Sebastopol to the allied camp, during the siege of that city, said, "*The place is a perfect hell!*" The historian of the "Thirty Years' War" thus depicts the condition of the public morals, both among the soldiery and the populace, during its continuance: "Such was the state of triumphant crime that many, driven to despair, denied even the existence of a Deity, declaring that if there were a God in heaven, he would not fail to destroy with thunder and lightning such a world of sin and wickedness."

And these evils are not confined to the seat of war, but extend to places more remote. The admiration of splendid military achievements; the pride of successful warfare, or the anger of defeat; the public gratulations and illuminations that celebrate every *brilliant* exploit, and testify the common joy over an unusually murderous victory; the popular thirst for military glory which is excited, and the sentiments of revenge everywhere nourished—all these tend to demoralize to an alarming degree the entire countries engaged in war.

Friends of virtue, lovers of morality, Christians, can you sanction this terrible source of iniquity? "*Shall the sword devour for ever?*"

III. Look at the DESTRUCTION OF DOMESTIC HAPPINESS caused by war.

It rudely summons men from their homes and firesides, and, regardless of the most tender relations of life and the claims of natural affection, bids them exchange scenes of endearing love for those of hate, and the charms of a happy fireside for long, weary marches, and exposure to the worst of deaths. It takes him whose manly strength is the support of a devoted family, in whom centre many affections and fond hopes, and who gives promise of long years of usefulness, and hurries him away to a work in which he cannot probably survive more than *three years*. Or it takes the son, whose budding manhood is the pride of many hearts, and tears him away with the prospect that he may never return, but die in a far-off land, cut down like a brute, with no fond eye to weep his untimely end, and no kind hand to bind up his wounds, or close his eyes, or perform for him the last sad offices of love.

Look at one of the ten thousand homes thus desolated by war. The wife broods over the absent one who has been ruthlessly snatched from her embrace, and perhaps plies wearily the needle to which she is compelled to resort for livelihood. The mother misses the familiar tones of her idolized son, whom she had hoped would be the staff of her old age. The prattling infants repeat with wondering anxiety the name of "father," and miss his accustomed caress. A shadow is upon every brow, and it is with sad misgivings that they await the intelligence from the seat of war, and pore over the accounts of *glorious victories* abroad. After months of agonizing suspense, they discover the name they love best among the "*killed.*" It becomes a house of mourning; the wife is a widow, and the children fatherless; their home is made desolate, and they perhaps become outcasts and wanderers in the world. They go abroad, weighed down under a life-long grief, unhappy monuments to the cruelty of that system which has deprived them of their heaven-provided guardian and protector. The *nation's* heart looks only upon the glory of a successful battle; or if it grieve at all over those who perished by it, its grief vanishes even more rapidly than the smoke from the battle-field. But no length of years can lift the pall from the hearts of the widowed and fatherless.

This is but a faint picture of the domestic desolations produced by a single battle in *thousands of homes.* The battle of Waterloo is said to have clothed no small part of England in mourning. Bourrienne says of Napoleon's campaign in Russia, "How many wives and mothers in France could not, without a palpitating heart, break the cover of the official gazette! How many families lost their support and their hope! Never were more tears shed. In vain did the cannon of the Invalides thunder forth the announcement of a victory. How many thousands, in the silence of retirement, were even then preparing the external symbols of mourning! It is still remembered that for the long space of six months the black dresses of Paris presented a very striking appearance in every part of the city." What a monstrous system of injustice is that which thus involves the innocent with the guilty, and for the sake of humbling a public enemy, cruelly rends the fondest ties of private life.

There are other devastations of the domestic hearth attendant upon a state of war which are of the most revolting character. The scenes of outrage which usually follow the capture of a town or city, are enough to make the blood run cold, and the whole frame shiver with horror. A writer, describing the bombardment of Vera Cruz by the United States troops in 1847, says, "I heard a great many heart-rending tales which were told by the survivors; but I have neither the inclination nor the time to repeat them. One, however, I will name. A French family were quietly seated in their parlor the evening previous to hoisting the white flag, when a shell from one of our mortars penetrated the building, and exploded in the room, *killing the mother and four children*, and wounding the residue." After the capture of the town of Kertch by the Allies, in 1855, it is related that Turkish stragglers and others "flocked into the town, and perpetrated the most atrocious crimes. To pillage and wanton devastation, they added violation and murder. One miscreant was shot as he came down the street in triumph, waving a sword wet with the blood of a poor child whom he had hacked to pieces. Others were slain in the very act of committing horrible outrages."

An instance of one home made desolate in our revolutionary war is heart-rending. It is the well-known case of Colonel Hayne. His wife and six children were still living when he was taken prisoner by the British and sentenced to be hung. His wife soon afterwards fell a victim to disease and grief. Strenuous efforts were made for his release, and his six motherless children knelt as suitors for their father's life, but in vain. His eldest son, a boy of thirteen, upon seeing his father loaded with irons, and condemned to the gallows, was overcome with grief, and throwing his arms around his neck, cried, "O my father, I will die with you—I will die with you, father!" The next morning he was led forth to execution. As they neared the gallows, he said to his son, who accompanied him, "Now, my son, show yourself a man. That tree is the boundary of my life and all its sorrows. Beyond that the wicked cease from troubling, and the weary are at rest. Don't lay our separation too much to heart—it will be short at longest. It was but the other day your dear mother died; to-day I die; and you, my son, though young, must follow shortly." "Yes, my father," replied the broken-hearted boy, "I shall follow you shortly, for I feel that indeed I can't, can't live long." His words were fulfilled. Upon seeing his father struggling in the death-agony upon the gallows, "he stood transfixed with horror. Till then he had all along wept profusely as some relief to his agonized feelings—but that sight! It dried up the fountain of his tears; he never wept again. His reason reeled upon the spot; he became an incurable maniac; and in his last moments he called out, and kept calling out for his father, in tones that drew tears from the hardest hearts."

Let such instances suffice to show the influence of war upon *the homes of the world.* Shall it continue thus to pollute and desecrate and destroy those shrines of the affections? Shall the heart's peculiar sanctuary be thus laid waste, and converted into a scene of fiendish outrage? Shall that system be any longer tolerated which invades the sacred precincts of the domestic hearth, and there immolates best-loved objects to this insatiate Moloch, cutting down valued and innocent lives, and breaking the hearts that loved them? "*Shall the sword devour for ever?*"

CHAPTER IX.

EVILS OF WAR—CONTINUED.

IV. LOOK at the PERSONAL SUFFERINGS OF THE BATTLE-FIELD.

These are beyond the power of imagination to conceive, or pen to describe. The effort to portray them has frequently been made, and the page of history is blackened with narrations of them which seem enough to dissolve the most hardened in tears. But no pen has ever painted a hundredth part of the sufferings that have been thus inflicted. We read the story of an engagement, of the number killed and wounded, and of the subsequent appearance of the field of conflict, and we perhaps drop a tear over the pathetic narrative, and turn from it shuddering with horror. Yet after all we have only a general view of the scene. The mind does not take in each particular pang of the sufferers, *nor can it.* By a merciful provision of our Creator, we cannot conceive of a tithe of that woe which, if vividly realized, would overwhelm us with unavailing sorrow.

Yet we should by no means close our eyes to it. It is one of the designs of Providence in forming our hearts tender and sympathizing, that they shall, by feeling for misery, be impelled to its alleviation.

Visit in imagination the field of battle. The chosen spot is perhaps one teeming with the fruits of successful industry. The calm stillness—the happy aspect of all nature—the cultivated fields—the waving harvests—the abounding thrift and plenty—the lowing herds—the shouts of husbandmen—the songs of birds and children—and the smiling cottages and gardens—all indicate the presence of love and *peace*. Presently the Sabbath-like quiet is broken by distant sounds of music. Upon either side it advances, and you soon hear the steady tramp of armies approaching in opposite directions. The flaunting plumes and banners, the forest of glistening bayonets, and the brilliant uniforms of a hundred thousand men, form an imposing spectacle, and the eye is dazzled by the serried array of splendors. A pause, and then they meet with a tremendous shock, and amid the roaring of cannon, and the rattling of musketry, fulfil the purpose which has brought them there. Balls and bombshells pass each other in the air with incredible rapidity. Some lose their heads, others their limbs, and at every exchange of shots hundreds are mangled and mutilated. As the foremost columns fall, others press on over their heaped-up bodies. Galloping war horses trample upon the wounded, or stumble over them and crush out their lingering lives. Ever and anon a shell explodes in the midst of a closely packed mass of human beings, and scatters them about in bloody fragments. Frenzied shrieks and groans fill the air, the discordant chorus being every moment augmented by the voices of new sufferers. And still on, and on, for hour after hour, rages the infernal work, with a power which is only limited by the deathful capacity of their weapons, or by the loss of hands to wield them.

At length one army or the other is *victorious*, and hostilities are for a while suspended. The smoke lifts itself slowly from the field—as if reluctant to unveil such carnage to the view of heaven—and you once more gaze upon the scene. How changed! Instead of the life-sustaining harvest, there is a harvest of death.

The cottages are burned, their inmates murdered, and sweet, innocent children lie weltering in their blood, or else cling, terrified and sobbing, to the lifeless forms of their parents. You go through the battle-field. Groans and outcries and mad blasphemies salute the ear on every side. Here lies one whose distorted features and pleading eye express the agony his lips refuse to utter. Here is a moving mass of beings, whom you would scarcely recognize as human, vainly endeavoring to extricate themselves from the pile or trench which has received them while yet living. Here is an unhappy wretch, clasping to his breast the picture of a loved wife or mother whom he will never behold again; another, frantic with agony, calling upon God to save his soul; another ending his tortures, now grown beyond endurance, by suicide; another, more timid, begging you to end them for him; another appealing piteously for water; another for help to move. There lies one whom pain has bereft of reason, and whose clinched hands, and glaring eye, and raving words proclaim him a maniac. Everywhere you behold men writhing under their sufferings of body and distractions of mind, and crying out, with frantic vehemence, to God and man for relief. But with most of them in vain. The hot sun beats upon them, or the cold storm pelts them, and thus they will lie, bleeding and helpless, until they die of their wounds or their exposure, or else of starvation.

And who are these visitors, picking their way among fallen bodies and scanning so eagerly their features? They are parents searching for their sons, wives for their husbands, and friends for friends. Ever and anon a mournful wail announces that some one has found the object of his search. Others are thieves and robbers, who unfeelingly strip the dying of their property, and only answer their entreaties and remonstrances with abuse or death. Birds of prey hover greedily about, and like many who swarm the field in human form, seize indiscriminately upon the living and the dead. What a concentration of unmitigated woe meets in the compass of a single battle-field! Is there any scene that so nearly resembles a hell on earth?

Perhaps we cannot better gain an idea of its sufferings than by glancing at those of one individual wounded in battle, and then multiplying them by ten, twenty, or fifty thousand. As an instance, take the statement of Sergeant Milton, who was wounded in the battle of Resaca de la Palma. Speaking of the celebrated charge of May's dragoons, he says, "At that moment a ball passed through my horse on the left side, and shattered my right leg. The shot killed the horse instantly, and he fell upon my left leg, fastening me by his weight to the earth. There I lay, right in the midst of the action, where carnage was riding riot, and every moment the shot, from our own and the Mexican guns, was tearing up the earth around me. I tried to raise my horse so as to extricate my leg, but I had already grown so weak with my wound that I was unable, and, from the mere attempt, I fell back exhausted. To add to my horror, a horse who was careering about riderless, within a few yards of me, received a wound, and commenced struggling and rearing with pain. Two or three times he came near falling on me, but at length, with a scream of agony and a bound, he fell dead, his body touching my own fallen steed. What I had been in momentary dread of now occurred—my wounded limb, which was lying across the horse, received another ball in the ankle. I now felt disposed to give up; and, exhausted through pain and excitement, a film gathered over my eyes, which I thought was the precursor of dissolution. . . . The tide of action now rolled away from me, and hope again sprung up. . . . . While I was thus nursing the prospect of escape, I beheld, not far from me, a villainous-looking *ranchero*, armed with an American sergeant's short sword, despatching a wounded American soldier, whose body he robbed. The next he came to was a Mexican, whom he served the same way; and thus I looked on while he murderously slew four. I drew an undischarged pistol from my holsters, and laying myself along my horse's neck, watched him, expecting to be the next victim; but something frightened him from his vulture-like business, and he fled in another direction. . . . Two hours after, I had the pleasure of shaking some of my comrades by the hand, who were picking up the wounded."

Again, then, survey the battle-field, and with this statement of a single wounded man for a clue, try to conceive of the aggregate pains of all the others. A writer describing the battle-field of Resaca de la Palma, says, "The evening closed on hundreds of them—the Mexicans—wounded, dying, and dead upon the field and on the road to the river. In the panic of flight, self-preservation was the single thought of each individual. The bleeding and the exhausted were borne down and forsaken by the sound and the strong. The parties on foot were trampled by the cavalry; and none of the multitude fleeing from their foes found help or comfort from their friends. The thickets and the hollows distant from the scene of strife, long afterwards told the story of many a wounded soldier who had struggled on to some secluded spot, there to linger, to thirst, to hunger, to bleed, to faint, and to perish alone in his long and varied agony."

The battle of Borodino, in which two hundred and sixty thousand men were engaged, is thus described by an eye-witness: "The fire of two hundred pieces of cannon enveloped the two armies in smoke, and mowing down whole battalions of men, strewed the field with the dead and wounded. The latter fell to expose themselves to a fate still more terrible. How agonizing their situation. Forty thousand dragoons, crossing the field in every direction, trampled them under foot, and dyed their horses' hoofs in their blood! The flying artillery, in rapid and alternate advance and retreat, put a period to the anguish of some, and inflicted new torments on others, who were mangled by their wheels. . . . Night separated the combatants, but left eighty thousand men dead on the field." In traversing the field the next day, he beheld "a surface of about nine miles square in extent covered with the killed and wounded." "But," he adds, "the most dreadful spectacle of all was the interior of the ravines, where the wounded had instinctively crawled to avoid the shot. Here these unfortunate wretches, lying one upon another, destitute of assistance, and weltering in their blood, uttered the most horrid groans. Loudly invoking death, they besought us to put an end to their excruciating torments."

The same writer, describing the sickening horrors that attended the entrance of the French troops to Moscow, says, "The hospitals, containing *more than twelve thousand wounded*, began at length to burn. The heart recoils at the disaster which ensued. Almost all those wretched victims perished! The few still living were seen crawling, half burnt, from the smoking ashes, or groaning under the heaps of dead bodies, and making ineffectual efforts to extricate themselves." A similar occurrence took place during the siege of Sebastopol, when a hospital of that city, said to have contained two thousand sick and wounded, was set on fire by the guns of the allies, and burned to the ground!

Mr. Russell, the London Times correspondent, thus describes the scenes subsequent to the battle of Inkermann, in which about eleven thousand were killed and wounded: "In every bush, on every yard of blood-stained ground, lay a dead or dying Russian. The British and the French, many of whom had been murdered by the Russians as they lay wounded, wore terrible frowns on their faces, with which the agonies of death had clad them. Some, in their last throes, had torn up the earth in their hands, and held the grass in their fingers up towards heaven. . . . But the wounded—for two long days they had lain where the hand and the ball had felled them. . . . The Russians, groaning and palpitating as they lay around,

were far more numerous. Some of these were placed together in heaps, that they might be the more readily removed. Others glared on you from the bushes, with the ferocity of wild beasts, as they hugged their wounds. Some implored in an unknown tongue, but in accents not to be mistaken, water, or succor—holding out their mutilated and shattered limbs, or pointing to the track of the lacerating ball."

The same writer thus describes the scene presented by the hospital of Sebastopol, immediately after its occupation by the allies: "Entering one of these doors, I beheld such a sight as few men, thank God, have ever witnessed. In a long low room, supported by square pillars, arched at the top, and dimly lighted through shattered and unglazed window frames, lay the wounded Russians, who had been abandoned to our mercies by their general. The wounded, did I say? No, but the dead, the rotten and festering corpses of the soldiers who were left to die in their extreme agony, untended, uncared for, packed as close as they could be stowed, some on the floor, others on wretched trestles and bedsteads, or pallets of straw, sopped and saturated with blood, which oozed and trickled through upon the floor, mingled with the droppings of corruption. With the roar of exploding fortresses in their ears, with shells and shot forcing through the roof and sides of the rooms in which they lay, with the crackling and hissing of fire around them, those poor fellows, who had served their loving friend and master the Czar but too well, were consigned to their terrible fate. Many might have been saved by ordinary care. Many lay, yet alive, with maggots crawling in their wounds. Many nearly mad by the scene around them, or seeking escape from it in their extremest agony, had rolled away under the beds, and glared out on the heart-stricken spectators, *O with such looks!* Many with legs and arms broken and twisted, the jagged splinters sticking through the raw flesh, implored aid, water, food, or pity; or, deprived of speech by the approach of death, or by dreadful injuries on the head or trunk, pointed to the lethal spot. Many seemed bent alone on making their peace with heaven. The attitudes of some were so hideously fantastic as to appal one by a sort of dreadful fascination. Could that bloody mass of clothing and white bones ever have been a human being, or that burnt black mass of flesh have ever had a human soul? It was fearful to think what the answer must be. . . . I confess it was impossible for me to stand the sight, which horrified our most experienced surgeons. . . . But what must the wounded have felt who were obliged to endure all this, and who passed away without a hand to give them a cup of water, or a voice to say one kindly word to them!"

In the Chinese insurrection, 1854–5, the city of Fuhshan, containing a population of six hundred thousand, was set on fire by the insurgents. The conflagration lasted three days, and *two hundred thousand people*, according to the Chinese estimate—which, however, may be an exaggerated one—were burned to death!

But we forbear. Enough has been said to give a faint picture of the personal sufferings entailed upon mankind by war. Edmund Burke has estimated the total loss of life by war at *thirty-five thousand millions.* O what tears and sighs and groans—what pains of body and griefs of mind—what crushed hopes—what bleeding, broken hearts, have attended the ravages of this cruel demon among so many of our race! We often shudder at the view of a single sufferer by disease or accident; and although he may be a stranger to us, shed tears of kindly sympathy for his woes. How, then, should we be affected by the view of *millions* writhing under tortures such as are rarely, if ever, witnessed in a peaceful land! There are many who weep profusely over the fictitious sufferings of imaginary heroes, when painted by a pathetic novelist. What scalding tears, then, should suffuse the eyes that read of War's *real* havoc! And here tears are manly, and it is weakness to withhold them. Upon such a subject as this, not to feel is to repudiate every higher instinct of our nature, and become worse than brutalized.

True, the view of such suffering is soul-harrowing and shocking to refined sensibilities; but shall we permit the evil to go unpitied and unalleviated *because it is so gigantic an evil?* Or perhaps there are some who, familiar with history and accustomed to such details, have ceased to be touched by them. Is it so, then, that the very *frequency* of this curse must render us insensible to it? Had there been but one or two battles in the world's history, they would be universally deplored; but because there have been thousands, they are regarded by many with indifference! Do we need any other proof of the evil of war than this—that *it has rendered it so common for men to suffer, that their sufferings almost cease to affect us?* The world has become, in this respect, very much like the experienced soldier, who, though once he would not knowingly have trampled upon an insect, is habituated to behold unmoved the most excruciating agonies of his fellow-men. Is it not time that we cast aside the stony exterior with which habit or prejudice has encrusted our hearts, and allow them to be impressed with those woes which are so well calculated to move them? "*Shall the sword devour for ever?*"

V. Prominent among the evils of war is the LOSS OF LIFE which it occasions.

The destruction of human life is its avowed object. It is with reference to this that weapons are invented and forged, and the most deadly forces of nature and art studied out and applied. Human ingenuity is tasked to its utmost to produce means which shall slay the greatest number of men with the most mathematical precision. The secrets of the earth are eagerly explored in the search for fatal agencies; and the murder of mankind upon a gigantic scale is made a science, whose study engages the attention of the profoundest intellects. Institutions whose sole object is the inculcating and perfecting of the art of killing men rapidly, gracefully, and scientifically, are supported at the public expense. Every military and naval academy might adopt, as expressing the whole scope of its instructions, the title of one of De Quincey's essays, "Murder considered as one of the Fine Arts." To this diabolical work every soldier is trained, and for this he is supported. This is the one great object of all his drills and reviews; and for this he is reduced to an "infernal machine," and divested of almost every thing human, excepting his vices, his power of motion, and his capacity for obeying orders. For this he is armed and led into battle, and the extent to which he there fulfils this murderous destiny so strongly inculcated upon him, is, to the warrior's view, the measure of his manhood. In expectation of this, hospitals are erected, and surgeons provided, and estimates calculated, like the following, which is quoted by Neckar, the French financier, from a state paper:

Forty thousand men to be embarked for the colonies, ...	40,000
To be deducted one-third for the first year's mortality, ...	13,333
Remainder, ...	26,667

The very idea of war unattended by great loss of life is an anomaly. The two are as inseparably connected as fire and burning, or poison and death, and none ever think of separating them.

As this is an evil which lies upon the surface, and is often the subject of statistical information, it is more generally recognized than any other. Yet how few reflect upon the true nature of this wholesale slaughter, or upon the dignity of its victims. Behold a *dying man*. For years he has walked the earth, one of the noblest of God's creatures. His exquisite organization—his intelligence—his comparative moral elevation—his immortal soul—all attest his towering dignity in the scale of being. Now he lies prostrate and helpless upon his couch. The darkened chamber—the attenuated form—the moans and gasps for breath—the numberless acts of tearful sympathy—proclaim the nearness of *death*. A struggle, and all is over. We bewail the mysterious providence, and think what a terrible curse is *sin*, that it should so rudely mar and destroy God's glorious creatures. Still more frightful does Death appear when the grim monster comes suddenly and unannounced, and, by what men call an *accident*, seizes his trophy from the walks of active life, and pales the cheek which but a moment since bloomed with the hue of abounding health! Clothed with yet darker horrors is the "last enemy" when he comes in the guise of the *assassin's* knife, and his victim is the prey of cold-blooded murder! With what indignation we try to ferret out the perpetrator of the crime, and bring him to justice and execution. And how, for years afterwards, we shudder at the bare remembrance of the deed!

Death, under all these circumstances, comes not with a tithe of the terrors which attend him upon the *battle-field*. There he is arrayed in his blackest garb, and invested with his most fearful and unalleviated horrors. He frowns on the expiring soldier with his most dreadful aspect. Every circumstance there conspires to aggravate the terrors of the dying hour, and accumulate around it all that can enhance its sting, while there is nothing to mitigate its utter dreariness. The soldier dies, not at home, and surrounded by sympathizing hearts, but amid unpitying strangers, whose every other instinct is absorbed in that of self-preservation; not by slow disease, upon a couch, with fond hands ministering to him, and all the appliances of medical skill about him, but butchered with bloody wounds, which none will bind up, and lying upon the hard cold ground; not, in most cases, summoned from the discharge of duties to God and man, and with the satisfaction of one who ends a well-spent life in the hope of a blessed immortality, but more often cut down in the commission of the grossest crime against God and his fellows, his arm brandishing the murderous weapon, which is perhaps already stained and dripping with human gore; not in the enjoyment of holy influences and means of grace, the man of God kneeling at his bedside, and his departing spirit commending itself to his Maker, but amid horrid blasphemies and imprecations; more than all, it is generally with no near prospect of heaven to rob death of its sting, for the Christian hope flies affrighted from the battle-field, and conducts few—alas, how few!—from the crimes of war to the bosom of the Prince of peace.

Now, bearing in mind these circumstances of fearful aggravation, consider the *vast numbers* who perish by such a death. It is impossible for the mind to embrace in a single view a distinct idea of death's ravages, when its victims are numbered by tens of thousands, as they have been in almost every battle of note whose details are recorded. This fact will perhaps account for the extraordinary indifference with which we read and hear of the losses of life by war. We dare not venture to grasp the tremendous thoughts suggested by such accounts, and so we spare ourselves almost all reflection upon the subject. This is wrong, and unworthy of rational, humane beings. Let us, then, look this evil in the face, until its view has inspired us with those emotions which are becoming to men, and to the partakers of this gift of life which is so worse than wasted.

Let us group together a few truthful statistics upon this subject, culled from the pages of history. At the battle of Austerlitz, 30,000 fell; at Jena and Lutzen, 30,000 each; at Eylau, 60,000; at Waterloo and Quatre Bras, 70,000; at Borodino, 80,000; at Fontenoy, 100,000; at Chalons, 300,000 of a single army. The Carthagenians attacked Hymera, Sicily, with an army of 300,000 men, and a fleet of 2,000 ships and 3,000 transports. "Not a ship or a transport escaped destruction; and of the troops, only a few in a small boat reached Carthage with the melancholy tidings." Marius slew in one battle 140,000 Gauls, and in another, 290,000. Tamerlane, in his camp before Delhi, massacred 100,000 Indian prisoners. "The people of Ispahan supplied him with 70,000 human skulls for the structure of several lofty towers, and a similar tax was levied by him upon Bagdad, amounting to 90,000 heads." Ghengis Khan slew 90,000 persons in cold blood on the plains of Nessa; at Herat, 1,600,000; and at Neisabar, 1,747,000. During the first fourteen years of his reign, he is supposed by Chinese historians to have destroyed eighteen millions, and in the last twenty-seven years, an average of more than half a million every year. This inhuman monster, whose wars were those of extermination, and whose armies sometimes exceeded a million, is said to have once "seriously proposed to exterminate all the inhabitants of China, that the vacant land might be converted to the *pasture of cattle*. The firmness of a Chinese mandarin alone diverted him from the execution of this horrible design." It is supposed that the whole number of souls that followed Xerxes into Greece was 5,283,320. Of these only 3,000 escaped destruction. Passing now to more modern times, it has been estimated that more than a million of lives were sacrificed in Napoleon's Russian campaign, which lasted only one hundred and seventy-three days, making an average of six thousand a day. Germany alone is said to have lost, in the Thirty Years' War, 12,000,000 of inhabitants. Not less than six millions perished by the wars of Napoleon in the heart of Christian Europe during the early part of this nineteenth century.

Terrible beyond conception have been the sufferings and deaths in besieged cities. In the siege of Paris, in the sixteenth century, 30,000 persons died of hunger alone. In the siege of Mexico, by the Spanish, more than

100,000 were slain in battle, and upwards of 50,000 more died from the infection of putrefying carcasses. The siege of Vienna destroyed 70,000; that of Ostend, 120,000; that of Acre, 300,000; that of Jerusalem, 1,100,000; and that of Troy, 1,816,000.

In our own day, the siege of Silistria, 1854, is said to have killed 30,000 Russians. The siege of Sebastopol, 1855, was attended with a fearful waste of life. During the last three weeks of that siege, the loss of the Russian garrison alone amounted to about 32,000, exclusive of those who perished by disease; and in the final assault, the south side of the city was taken at a loss, upon both sides, of at least 30,000. The total loss of life in the Crimea, from the landing of the Allies at Eupatoria to the fall of Sebastopol—a period of about one year—is estimated at 450,000.

In connection with these statements, must be borne in mind war's *indirect havoc*. In the Peninsular war in Spain, only 40,000 soldiers were killed or died of wounds received in battle; while 120,000 died of disease, and 120,000 more were by disease unfitted for service. During the first five years that the French were in

Algiers, their annual loss averaged about 5,000 by shot, and 15,000 by disease. In the war between the United States and Mexico, there were, to every American killed in battle, more than five who died from diseases incident to the climate and the camp. The ravages of disease among the allied armies in the Crimea, in 1854, were truly frightful. Says a letter writer: "Oct. 30. Cholera is committing its fatal ravages. Not a day passes without three or four of the officers, and about two hundred of the men being carried off by this terrible disease. Two days ago, not less than 16,000 men were on the sick-list, out of an army of now nearly 30,000. Dec. 3. The Turkish garrison at this place—Balaklava—are dying off at the rate of some one hundred and fifty a day. It is not at all uncommon to see the corpses of these unfortunate beings, who have been stricken down by cholera on their way to the hospital, lying along the road-side. . . . . The sick appear to be tended by the sick, and the dying by the dying." It was stated that the number of Russian invalids throughout the Crimea in June, 1855, amounted to 100,000. The typhus-fever, which broke out at Sebastopol in the spring of that year, carried off very many.

Taking into consideration the numbers who have fallen in battle, and those who have perished by the more remote ravages of war, we shall be prepared to assent to the estimate of Dr. Dick, that more than fourteen thousand millions of human beings, or one tenth of the human race, have been thus slaughtered since the beginning of the world. Edmund Burke, as has been already said, places the number still higher, making it thirty-five thousand millions; and others have even reckoned it at twice that sum, or seventy thousand millions. Of course the amount defies all efforts at accurate computation; but taking the estimate of Burke as near the truth, we find that the loss by war has been *thirty-five times the entire present population of the globe!* Suppose it were known that thirty-five worlds such as ours had been suddenly destroyed, with all their inhabitants, what a wail of agony would rend the universe, and how all living creatures would be bowed down with grief! How, then, should the view of an equal number of beings mutually slaughtered upon this earth affect us? And all these victims were human, formed to love God and their fellows, and possessed of immortal souls. And they have been mowed down, not by fiends and demons, but by *men.* For nearly every death we must behold a human hand imbrued in blood, and a human heart defiled with murder. "*Shall the sword devour for ever?*"

VI. The most appalling of all the evils of war is its DESTRUCTION OF SOULS.

As the soul's life is of inconceivably greater value than that of the body, and as the sufferings of eternity immeasurably surpass those of time, we must look for the chief havoc of war in its eternal effects upon men's higher and spiritual nature. To the view of the Christian, its greatest outrages are those which here lie hid from public observation, and which only future and everlasting ages can disclose. They are too terrible for protracted contemplation, and we shall but briefly hint at them. Indeed, it is from the nature of the case impossible to give more than their dim outline. The sad experience of the soul's ever-living, never-ending death can alone fill up the picture.

Without pausing to notice the barriers which war opposes to the conversion of the multitudes in warring countries—and they are mighty—let us confine our view to its destruction of souls among the actual combatants. It tends, as we have already seen, to the demoralization of all those who engage in it. While it does not inculcate or call into exercise a single virtue, it teaches and inculcates almost every vice; and in the proportion in which it influences men, generally hardens their hearts, and renders their salvation more and more improbable. As commonly engaged in, it is the service of Belial, and "no man can serve two masters." What two things can be more incompatible than religion and murder? What; loving and obeying God, yet openly and habitually violating his plain command, "Thou shalt not kill?" Loving one's neighbor as himself, yet butchering him in cold blood! A disciple of the meek and lowly Jesus, yet burning with fury and resentment! The thought is absurd and inconsistent to the last degree. That religion may exist in the soldier's camp, we by no means deny. But even if some earnestly pious souls, through either a real or mistaken patriotism, or by the force of circumstances, engage in war, to what temptations they must become exposed. Truly that is a strong, *real* piety which can survive the scoffs and ribaldry which assail it among men who hold every Christian virtue in contempt, defy their Maker, and glory in the rivalry of irreligion.

Admitting, however, that there have been many who have carried even a saving religion into the camp and battle-field, and casting over their inconsistencies the mantle of charity, we must still ask, whither go *the unnumbered multitudes* of war's votaries? Ah, let the voice of God reply: "*No murderer hath eternal life abiding in him.*" The alternative is eternal death. Dismal are the sufferings of the battle-field, with its restless agonies and vain cravings of hunger and thirst, but they are not to be compared with the gnawings of the undying worm, and that spirit's thirst which no drop of water shall ever quench. Dreadful is war's havoc of *bodily* life, but it becomes insignificant by the side of its destruction of those many *souls* whom it plunges into irremediable wretchedness.

This most fearful of all war's ravages is unappreciated by the world, but Christians know something of the worth of the soul, and of the tremendous interests that are involved in its salvation or damnation. Christians know that all the united kingdoms and thrones, and wealth and glory, for which so many have been sacrificed, are, when weighed against one human soul, but as the dust of the balance. For long after the fashion of this world has passed away, and this blood-stained earth has been burned up, and the causes and temporal results of war have been forgotten like a dream, the souls whom it has ruined shall weep and wail *for ever.* O Christian, shall this curse continue to scathe the moral world, to pollute and destroy unnumbered deathless spirits, and in depopulating earth to people hell? "*Shall the sword devour for ever?*"

VII. We shall conclude our view of the evils of war with noticing its OBSTACLES TO THE SPREAD OF THE GOSPEL AND THE TRIUMPH OF CHRISTIANITY.

The church of Christ is becoming every year more alive to her proper work of evangelizing the world, and is beginning to appreciate her high privilege as honored with an embassy of peace to all men. Beautiful is the contrast she presents to those whose destructive ravages we have just contemplated. Her war is not against man, but for man and against his common enemy. "We wrestle not with flesh and blood." The "sacramental host of God's elect" battles with error, idolatry, strife, and crime. It achieves bloodless conquests, and its weapon, "the sword of the Spirit," "mighty through God," is already wresting large provinces from Satan's empire, and annexing them to the dominions of the Prince of peace. But the church has something more to do than the sending out of Bibles and missionaries, before her *whole* work can be accomplished. There are obstacles to be overcome, stumbling-blocks to be removed, objections and cavillings to be silenced, and glaring inconsistencies to be done away. If the Redeemer is to come upon earth in the power and glory of his spiritual kingdom, the voice must be heard and heeded throughout all Christendom, "*Prepare ye the way of the Lord, make his paths straight.*"

An indispensable step towards securing the triumph of the gospel, is the abolition of war. This practice, together with its other evil effects, fetters religious effort, and impedes the progress of Christianity. •Besides its disastrous influences upon the public morality in the so called Christian nations, it opposes a formidable barrier to the reception of the Bible in heathen lands. Its effect upon the mind of a reasoning idolater may readily be imagined. He says to himself, "This gospel is good; its precepts are wise and beautiful; and had it reached me from any other source, I should gladly receive and obey it. But it comes to me from a *Christian* nation which, while professing to conform to it, yet engages in a practice which it forbids, and that, too, in a manner which seems barbarous even to me, whom they call a barbarian. Now either Christianity is not true, or these nations are not Christian. Let them drop their name, or their cruel contentions, and I will listen to them."

Thus reasoned the natives of India, who had witnessed the bloody conquests, and then the mutual slaughter of the English, French, Dutch, and Portuguese upon their soil. "If *this* be Christianity," said they, "we want no such bloody religion." The famous wall of China opposed no such barrier to the reception of the gospel into that empire, as was raised by the conduct of nominal Christians. When the missionaries first applied for admission there, the emperor sternly refused, "for," said he, "*wherever Christians go, they whiten the soil with human bones.*" A Turk at Jerusalem once asked a missionary, "Why do you come here?" He replied, "To bring you peace." "*Peace!*" rejoined the Turk, with a contemptuous sneer. Leading the missionary to a window, he pointed to Calvary. "There," said he, "upon the very spot where your Lord poured out his blood, the Mohammedan is obliged to interfere to prevent *Christians* from shedding the blood of one another." Our missionaries have been of late years successfully teaching gospel truths in Turkey. The poor Mohammedans listened eagerly to the simple and sublime precepts, and they were winning with gentle force upon their hearts, when suddenly they were summoned forth to defend their country against the savage onsets of a nominally Christian nation, while they beheld the allied armies of two other Christian nations awaiting the given signal to deluge Europe with Christian blood. Well might they have asked, "Is this the gospel of love? Are these the servants of the Prince of peace? We will follow Mohammed, and thus, if wrong in some things, at least be consistent." May not such reflections as these naturally arise, and shed a ray of delusive light upon the mind of the serious inquirer after truth, betraying him to ruin? His argument is not indeed a just one; but there are few pagan minds so discriminating as to distinguish, at first view, between real and nominal Christianity, or to receive God's word solely upon its own merits, and independently of the example of Bible-reading nations.

In many portions of the globe, the cause of Christ has been in this manner greatly prejudiced. The wars of the British in China and Affghanistan, those of the French in Africa, and those of the United States on the Indian frontiers—all conducted upon the very soil where Christians were planting the gospel banner—must have left impressions highly unfavorable to Christianity, and which it may require long years of peace to efface.

We have presented but a single aspect of this alarming evil, yet perhaps the most striking one. Others will readily suggest themselves to the reflecting mind. It will be considered that war deals a powerful blow at those agencies by which the work of missions is carried on; that it absorbs resources which might otherwise have been devoted to this grand enterprise; that it diverts from it, or destroys men who might otherwise engage in it; and that even the small measure of success which is permitted to us will be, at best, the spreading abroad of a defective Christianity.

Is it objected that we are viewing the church as responsible for the crimes of the ungodly? To some extent, she is so; for who can believe that Christians could not, long before this, have lifted up such an earnest and powerful voice against war, as would have driven it from their own countries, and rendered peace the invariable fruit and attendant of civilization? It would require but a few efforts of the united evangelical world to sheathe every sword of Christendom in its scabbard, and confine this "trade of barbarians"—as even Napoleon termed it—to those "dark places of the earth" and "habitations of cruelty," where alone it appropriately belongs. And is not the church accountable to God for so long withholding those efforts?

Then let all who pray, "Thy kingdom come," unite for removing this obstacle from "the way of the Lord." Let the church arise, and shake off this monstrous enemy who has long enough pinioned her to the dust, and sown the tares of discord and violence in the field of the world. And let the church enlist upon her side that powerful ally provided in the gospel, which, though so long stifled and neglected, is now beginning to assert its might, and let the cause of *missions* and of *peace* go hand in hand, for they are one. Let Christianity be commended to human hearts by a practical demonstration of its divine principles. Then it will carry conviction to many minds, and the nations will the more cordially embrace the *religion of love.*

CHAPTER X.

PLEAS FOR WAR CONSIDERED.

It would seem as if it were hardly necessary to present any other argument against war than is afforded by the view of its evils. This is one of those subjects upon which the mere feelings and natural emotions of the humane mind form argument enough. To one who honestly contemplates this dire curse, slow processes of reasoning seem uncalled for. It appears much as if men were to argue earnestly before a civilized community to show that cannibalism, or the Hindoo suttee, is both cruel and wicked. We believe the time will come when we shall no more require argument upon the one subject than upon the others. But there are now those who defend war as just and necessary. Many of them are intelligent, their number is by no means small, and their opinions are entitled to a respectful consideration. We shall therefore notice a few of the more prominent pleas for war, and then apply to the system the test of both reason and revelation.

I. It is affirmed that war is necessary as a means of REDRESS FOR NATIONAL GRIEVANCES. How else, it is asked, shall we find relief from wrong and oppressive conduct, or bring a foe who has injured us to a reparation of his fault? These questions we hope to answer in a subsequent chapter, where we shall exhibit what we conceive to be the *Right Way* of redressing grievances. It will be sufficient for our present purpose to show that, as a general thing, *war does not* accomplish this desired end.

Suppose that one nation has grossly insulted or trampled upon the rights of another. The aggrieved government feels that its honor or prosperity is at stake, and that some means must be employed to vindicate the one, or defend the other. Custom places before it but one alternative—it must either suffer the wrong, or else, by force of arms, compel its reparation. If it is weak in proportion to its foe, and there is a moral certainty of its defeat, it of necessity opposes no resistance—and where then is its *redress?* If, however, it is of such comparative strength in fleets and armies as to seem able to cope in battle with its adversary, it appeals to arms, issues the declaration of war, arouses the popular indignation and thirst for vengeance, summons its citizens to leave their peaceful homes and arm for the conflict, and invades the enemy's country. Battle after battle is fought, brilliant victories are achieved, and blood is poured out like water. At length, both parties becoming wearied of the struggle, they begin to discuss the terms of peace. A treaty is formed, amicable relations restored, armies recalled and disbanded, and every thing settles down to its accustomed quiet.

Now what has been gained? *Redress?* If it so chanced that the offended party was at the same time the more powerful one, and possessed the most skilful generals, it has probably compelled those injuring it to make some kind of reparation. Yet even supposing such to have been the case, and that it has even acquired in territory and power far more than it demanded at the outset, we still ask, *what has been gained?* A favorable decision of a vexed question, which turned perhaps upon a mere technicality, or a few square miles of territory, and the public applause—and to gain these it has sacrificed millions of money, subjected itself to repeated indignities and losses, and shed the blood of thousands of its subjects. What has been gained? Burdens of debt, and yet heavier burdens of iniquity, broken hearts, desolated homes, widows and orphans, poverty, crime, and death. *Who shall redress all these?* Who shall repair the evils inflicted by the government upon its own subjects? By what means shall the guiltless inhabitants of either country be compensated for *their* losses? Surely, if war be the proper mode of national redress, it is the same for individuals; and who could complain if the outraged communities should give battle to their own governments, which had proved a greater enemy to them than any foreign power, and insist upon butchering their rulers, in order to repair the wrongs committed against themselves? We believe it may be confidently asserted that there has never been a war—excepting perhaps those that were strictly defensive—whose gain has equalled its losses, or in which the amount of justice and happiness secured, or wrong rectified, has equalled the degree of guilt and misery incurred. So that even supposing the particular end in view to have been attained, it is more than outweighed by its cost of life, happiness, and prosperity. It is as if two neighbors, who had quarrelled, should array their respective families against each other in deadly conflict. What kind of *redress* has the injured one obtained when, for a few dollars, or a trifling piece of ground, he has sacrificed his beloved children, and clouded for life both his home and his heart?

Well said Cicero, "The worst peace is preferable to the best war;" and Franklin, whose economical maxims are so much practised by individuals, gave one well worthy of a nation's study when he said, "Whatever advantage one nation would obtain from another, it would be cheaper to purchase such advantage with ready money, than to pay the expenses of acquiring it by war."

It is not true, however, that in general redress is thus obtained, or justice secured. The "chances of war" have passed into a proverb. There is no more likelihood of its resulting in favor of the right than the drawing of lots would be, nor indeed as much. For it is usually the case that a nation is careful to injure only those who are weaker than itself, and who, if they resist at all, seem likely to become its easy prey. In almost every instance of national oppression, the victims are less powerful than the aggressors, and their injuries would be rather increased than lessened by war. And even if the two powers appear to be equally balanced, an appeal to arms is as likely to result in favor of the one as the other, there being ten thousand little, unforeseen circumstances which may turn the tide of victory. There is no necessary connection between justice and military success. God has not ordained that the right shall always be proved and vindicated by battle. Many seem to view it as of a nature with the Urim and Thummim of the Jewish high-priest, or as the ancient mode of judicial combat was regarded—something presided over by the divine Providence for the purpose of infallibly pointing out the right. With far more show of reasonableness the nations might decide their disputes by a throw of the dice, solemnly appealing to God to indicate the right. How precarious is the chance of *redress* in a practice which is so proverbially the creature of "fortune" and accident, as even Napoleon acknowledged war to be.

Experience has not only proved all this, but also that war, when it does not greatly complicate the difficulties, and render their adjustment yet more arduous, generally *leaves the point at issue where it found it*, and that the contending nations are compelled finally to negotiate upon the subject just as they would if there had been no war. Thus in the last war between the United States and Great Britain, this country expended its three hundred millions of dollars, lost thousands of citizens, and inflicted a blow upon her own civil and commercial interests, from which it took her long to recover; and what was the result? After two years and a half of hostilities, a treaty of peace was concluded, which *left the controverted point*—the British impressment of American seamen—*precisely where the war first found it.* It is needless to multiply instances. The fact is well known that war, unless gaining its end by brute force—which has no connection whatever with right and justice—generally leaves the alleged grievance in its original position; and that redress, if obtained at all, is then gained by means of negotiation or arbitration, *which could just as well have been resorted to in the first instance.*

II. Another plea for war is, that A PACIFIC POLICY WOULD EXPOSE THE NATION TO YET GREATER INJURIES.

This difficulty, we conceive, exists only in imagination. Most certainly it cannot be proved true from the history of any nation, while much of individual experience proves quite the contrary. As has been shown in the former part of this work, and as must be evident to the observing mind, a forbearing spirit and conduct is generally attended with far greater safety than its opposite. This is as true of large bodies of men as it is of individuals. The resentful nation, like the resentful man, is always embroiling itself in new strifes, and literally inviting injuries; while the one which habitually forgives, and returns good for evil, *could such a one be found,* would be seen to be favored of God and man, and to possess, in its very forbearance, a more powerful means of defence than could be afforded by all the forts and armies and navies of the world. As has been said of individuals, so we may assert of nations, that none should employ this argument until they have at least attempted the experiment of an entirely pacific policy. It is a reproach to

Christendom that in the lapse of eighteen centuries so few trials of it have been made.

Happily, however, history is not without instances of the security of the right way, when practised upon this large scale. A more convincing demonstration of it could hardly be desired than is afforded by the early and well known history of Pennsylvania. To the astonishment of many in England, William Penn, with a small colony of Friends, planted himself in the midst of the most warlike tribes in America, with no other weapons than the principles of the gospel of peace. All predicted their speedy destruction. "What," said Charles II. to him, "venture yourself among the savages of North America! Why, man, what security have you that you will not be in their war-kettle within two hours after setting your foot on their shores?" "The best security in the world," replied the undaunted hero. "I doubt that, friend William," replied the king; "I have no idea of any security against these cannibals but a regiment of good soldiers, with their muskets and bayonets; and I tell you beforehand, that with all my good-will for you and your family, to whom I am under obligations, I will not send a single soldier with you." "I want none of the soldiers; I depend on something better." "Better? on what?" "*On the Indians themselves, on their moral sense, and on the promised protection of God.*" His prayer was, "Let the Lord guide me by his wisdom, to honor his name and serve his truth and people, *that an example and a standard may be set up to the nations.*" "*There may be room there,*" said he, "*though not here, for the holy experiment.*" Now mark the result of that experiment. In the words of the Edinburgh Review, speaking of Penn's treaty with the Indians, "Such indeed was the spirit in which the negotiation was entered into, and the corresponding settlement conducted, that for the space of more than seventy years, so long indeed as the Quakers retained the chief power in the government, the peace and amity which had been thus solemnly promised and concluded, never was violated; and a large, though solitary example was afforded of the facility with which they who are really sincere and friendly in their views, may live in harmony with those who are peculiarly fierce and faithless."

This is the only instance, so far as we are

aware, in which a government—for although a colony of Great Britain, it was to the Indians as an independent state—has publicly recognized and practised the duty of a literal obedience to the gospel precepts. The complete success which crowned that obedience is a triumphant vindication of its efficacy. In the midst of six warring nations, who had the most bitter hostility to the whites, and whose prejudices against them had been strengthened by all their previous intercourse, separated by the broad Atlantic from their mother country, without arms, and with no show of defence whatever, they remained uninjured as long as they adhered to their pacific policy. The ferocious savage, who was the incessant terror of the other colonies, became the friend and powerful ally of this one. The tomahawk and scalping-knife, so often imbrued in the blood of armed settlers, were sacredly withheld from the defenceless Quakers; and when, in a few instances, some of them were killed, the savages humbly apologized with the words, "The men *carried arms*, and we supposed them to be fighters."

This only known instance, then, of a rigid

adherence to the right way, so far from exposing the community to injury, proved its best safeguard, and secured for it both outward respect and forbearance, and a high degree of internal prosperity. All honor to those who were the first to put in practice upon a large scale these gospel precepts, and who, in the heart of a savage wilderness, dared to work out for the world's study and imitation so glorious an example of obeying God. Would that to America it might be given again and yet more signally to illustrate the same sublime principles, and become to the nations of the earth a model not only of civil freedom, but also of that *moral* independence which will not brook the tyranny of war. She would be as successful and influential in the one as she is in the other; and the Providence that has so prospered her while erring, would not leave her a prey to her enemies while acting the part of a Christian people.

Besides, it may be confidently affirmed that the path of duty is always, more than any other, the path of security, and that they who the most conform to the divine will are the best entitled to look for the divine blessing and protection. It may with truth be said of nations as it is of individuals, that when their ways please the Lord, he maketh even their enemies to be at peace with them. See Prov. 16 : 7; 20 : 22, and 1 Pet. 3 : 13. This fact is happily illustrated in the history of the ancient Jews. God commanded that all their males should appear before him three times a year, promising them, at the same time, a security from hostile invasions during their attendance upon the required worship. "Neither," said He, "shall any man desire thy land, when thou shalt go up to appear before the Lord thy God thrice in the year." Ex. 34 : 23, 24. "It is a well-known fact," remarks Bishop Horne, "that the Jews constantly attended these feasts without fear of any danger, and that their most vigilant enemies never invaded or injured them during these sacred seasons." Thus our duty is ever our best interest; and were the experiment to be made, in this or any land, of a literal, fearless obedience to the gospel, all reason and experience, and the very nature of the divine government, assure us that it would be crowned with success.

III. One of the most frequent and plausible

pleas for war is, that it is sometimes necessary in order to SELF-DEFENCE. "Is it our duty," it may be asked, "to surrender our liberties and lives to the encroachments of an enemy without a struggle?" No: when these are at stake, and our soil is invaded by a foreign foe, it is right to protect them, and repel the enemy, if needs be, by force. In making this concession, however, we ask, How many of the wars of history have been defensive? This is, indeed, often their pretext, but its falsehood is apparent in almost every instance.

This very plea of self-defence implies a war of attack and invasion. The abolition of *all war* would abolish this only necessity for war; for in doing away with that which is *aggressive*—whose injustice all must admit—it would also take away every occasion for *defence*. So that even allowing this plea all the weight that is claimed for it, it still affords no objection to the general abolition of war and disarming of the nations, but rather an argument in its favor. Is it sometimes necessary that an invading foe be repelled by force of arms? It will be seen at once how this very fact implies that other necessity of the mutual abolition of this iniquitous practice; for when peace is once made the law of all the nations, and the armies are disbanded, there will be *no invasions to resist, and no attacks from which to defend ourselves.*

Besides, who knows what the effect would be, if a declaration of war were met with a spirit of forbearance, and kind efforts at conciliation, instead of bitter retorts and bristling bayonets? Let any nation make peace its avowed policy, and resolve never to fight except when the evil resisted is greater than would be entailed by war, and after having patiently endeavored to defend itself by other means; and it will probably shame its adversaries from their hostility, or weary them of the unequal and disgraceful conflict. The considerations already advanced, and the only experience to which we can point—that of the colony of Pennsylvania—leave it at least questionable whether the most savage of nations would give an unarmed, yet kind and forbearing people, any occasion for war.

IV. Another plea for war is, that it is sanctioned by time-honored CUSTOM. It has been the practice of nations ever since their existence, and shall we boast of being wiser than our fathers?

It is indeed an institution venerable with years; but so is idolatry, and vice and crime of every description; and the argument, in order to hold good, should defend them all alike. If war be a cruel, unjust, and inefficacious mode of settling national differences, then the fact that it has been long persisted in, so far from rendering it otherwise, only makes its present practice the more unreasonable. By having been so customary in all past ages, *it has given the world ample opportunities to test its efficacy.* From the very fact that it has been so generally engaged in, it has been for ages sounding in the ears of man its lessons of bitter experience. Shall we now refuse to heed those lessons, and casting down Example from her true office as a teacher, enthrone her as a tyrant? Shall we persist in a custom whose every repetition affords a fresh argument against itself? To do this would be to act unworthily of rational beings, to cast aside all manly independence, and to become fettered slaves to fashion. This principle, if fully carried out, would abolish Christianity from the face of the globe, and inthral mankind in sin more deeply than they now are. It is the argument of a bad cause, and its very weakness condemns the system in whose favor it is enlisted. The fact that it is made use of at all, reveals the degradation to which war has reduced its advocates. It is customary, say they, to butcher human beings, to burn villages, to demoralize whole countries, and to peril the eternal interests of large numbers of our fellow-men—"*customary, and therefore right!*" But it is sufficient to exhibit this plea; we need not dwell upon it.

V. It is a popular plea for war, that INSULTED HONOR often requires it. This is only another form of the absurd and unchristian maxim of the duellist, which is now generally exploded in the more enlightened circles of society. It means that any real or imagined indignity to that most delicate and sensitive of objects, a nation's flag, cannot be allowed to go unpunished, without branding with public disgrace every individual over whom that flag may wave.

Supposing, however, that a real injury has been inflicted—which is the most calculated to tarnish the national escutcheon, a forgiving, or a resentful course of conduct? Which best displays true greatness—an impetuous descent to the base level of the offender, or a magnanimous rising above it? It is the glory of a wise nation, as well as of a wise man, "to pass over a transgression." No reproach, either of a nation or of an individual, is ever wiped out with blood. The murder only plunges its perpetrator from a fancied dishonor to the depths of real infamy. "Could I wipe your blood from my conscience as easily as I can wipe this insult from my face," said a marshal of France, with a greatness to which he had never attained on the field of battle, "I would have laid you dead at my feet." True honor is not a thing which may be sullied by the indignities of others. Christ possessed his in all its transparent purity while the multitude were reviling and buffeting him. Had he resented their insults, then, and then only, his character would have been tarnished. So a nation maintains its honor just so long as it is guilty of no wrong actions, and no degree of injury or disrespect can deprive her of it; but the moment she stoops to retaliate abuse, and engage in the crime of murder, she becomes disgraced, and ought to be so regarded by every true man.

VI. There lies at the foundation of all these

pleas for war the general one of a mistaken PATRIOTISM.

Real patriotism we would by no means undervalue. The love of one's country and its preference to every other, is only just and natural. But who best displays a love for his country, and a regard for its honor and prosperity—he who aids in plunging it into war, and thus perils or destroys its highest interests, or he who strives by temperate efforts to avert so great a calamity? Although, in his enthusiastic ardor, a subject may be willing to pour out his blood for the fancied honor of his nation, is not such a patriotism apt to be the result of excited passion, rather than of cool reflection? The *true* patriot loves his country too well to countenance those crimes against God which are sure to bring upon it the divine judgments; and though willing himself to perish, if needs be, in defence of lives that are dear to him, is unwilling *needlessly* to sacrifice them to vengeance or ambition.

Patriotism has been made the pretext for much that deserves the name of narrow-minded selfishness and bigotry. The love of one's country does not necessarily demand a hatred of every other, nor a wanton disregard of their interests. Neither reason nor Scripture justify us in bounding our love to men by the narrow limits of our national territory. They alike bid us love and benefit all mankind, irrespective of country, latitude, or creed. The true Christian is a citizen of the world, and he is the best of all patriots, because his sympathies extend so widely. Yet there are those who inculcate, under the specious guise of patriotism, an inordinate attachment to the institutions of our native land, to the despising of every other; and who denounce as traitors those who will not, upon slight occasions, take up arms against a foreign power. They are themselves traitors to humanity. In so exalting the lesser bond of country, they forget the higher and more sacred one of the family of man. In the parable of the good Samaritan, our Lord rebukes this narrow policy, and inculcates love and kindness, not only to those of a different creed, but even to those of a hostile nation. A failure to conform to these teachings has done much towards encouraging a false patriotism, and has impelled many an enthusiast into the battle-field with the motto,

"Our country, *right or wrong*." When will men learn that humanity and religion are before patriotism, and the law of universal love before that of allegiance to one's country? Well said an eloquent American statesman, "Remember that you are men by a more sacred bond than you are citizens; and that you are children of a common Father more than you are Americans." There is a patriotism that is far above the love of any one earthly country; it is that which, overleaping all boundaries of kindred, sect, tribe, or nation, feels the woes of common humanity, and girds on the gospel armor to do battle against them. It is that which arrays itself against the moral tyrants of the world, and repels the invaders Strife and Passion, who have so long robbed us of our rightful liberties. All the world is the Christian's country, and all mankind, of every race and clime, are his fellow-citizens. No man is under such strong obligations to defend his native land from human foes, as he is to defend the world from the inroads of hell's armies. Against these let us unite our forces; and let every Christian, every philanthropist, every man arise, and in the strength of God battle to the death against the demon *War.* This would be a *patriotism* worthy of the name.

VII. There are those who attempt to derive a plea for war from THE BIBLE. "God commanded it to the Israelites," say they; "and in so doing, did He not sanction it for all succeeding time?"

This argument, like all others adduced by the advocates of war, is in the face of the general spirit of Christianity. As has been shown, the gospel forbids all unnecessary strife, and demands the exercise of love, forgiveness, and forbearance towards enemies. With that gospel before us, is it more than just to conclude that no previous commands of God can militate against it; and that, although unable to reconcile it with all the divine dealings, we must still *obey* precepts so plain and indisputable? Those precepts, too, are addressed directly to us. What right, then, have we to go back to commands given to the Jews alone, for the standard of our duty?

The plea is, however, a fallacious one. The wars of the Jews to which it refers, differed in many important particulars from any that have since been undertaken. Their great distinguishing feature is the one under consideration. They were sanctioned by divine authority, *and this cannot positively be affirmed of any other wars.* And does not the very fact that God deemed it necessary to *command* them, upon the occasions referred to, seem to imply that they would have been, under other circumstances, unlawful? Had it been right that they should engage in war without his especial sanction, we may suppose that he would have left them to do so, in conformity to the general custom of that age, and merely presided over their battles, and conducted them to a successful issue. God, however, the Creator of men, punishes and destroys them in many ways which it would be wrong for man to imitate. When, for wise reasons, He bid the Israelites become his instruments for punishing the idolatrous nations, he did that which, while perfectly just in him, would be unjust and criminal in us. When the divine command can again be proved with regard to any particular war, it will be our religious duty to obey it. Meantime we must require something more than the plea under consideration to justify a system which is opposed to the whole tenor of the gospel.

CHAPTER XI.

WAR TESTED BY REASON.

WHILE every plea that can be urged in defence of the practice of war is insufficient, there are the strongest arguments against it. We shall first apply to it the test of reason, and then consider the authoritative argument from revelation.

I. We affirm that war is, in general, UNNECESSARY. As has already been observed, those wars which are in the strictest sense of the term defensive, are no doubt unavoidable. With these single and rare exceptions, however, there are none which are demanded by the actual necessities of the combatants. In order to prove them otherwise, it must be shown that they are the only means of averting fatal calamities, that they remove evils greater than themselves, and that they procure good which is absolutely indispensable, and which could not be obtained in any other way. Those who look at the common causes and results of war, must admit that there are few, if any, of which all this can truly be said. A careful investigation into the occasions of two hundred and eighty-six great and bloody wars, instituted by the Massachusetts Peace Society, ascertained the following to be their origin: "Twenty-two for plunder or tribute; forty-four for the extension of territory; twenty-four for retaliation or revenge; six about disputed boundaries; eight respecting points of honor or prerogative; five for the protection or extension of commerce; fifty-five civil wars; forty-one about contested titles to crowns; thirty under pretence of assisting allies; twenty-three from mere jealousy of rival greatness; twenty-eight religious wars, including the crusades; *not one for defence alone.*" Now who will say that one of these wars was *necessary?* It is not necessary to plunder mankind, nor to extend territory, nor to retaliate injuries, nor thus to extend commerce, nor to sacrifice subjects to the rival claimants of a crown; nor is that religion necessary which is enforced at the point of the sword or bayonet. None of these are indispensable to men's existence—none of them such wants as to justify this means of satisfying them. But *it is necessary* that men should live, that God should be obeyed, that crime should be avoided, and that souls should not be trained for perdition, and then hurried into it.

The very nature of war proves that there can be little if any real necessity for it; for what evil is so great that this one can relieve, instead of augmenting it? What curse so dire, that this one must be embraced as its only and better alternative? Is it possible for either rulers or subjects to be reduced to such extremities that only streams of human blood can relieve them? Ah, sin has caused many an evil to our race, but none that requires so terrible a remedy. It has not brought us to such straits that war is become one of the necessaries of life. Men have suffered for the want of Christian kindness and forbearance, and for the want of peace, but never for want of war. They have suffered for the want of virtue, holiness, and happiness, but never for want of misery, crime, and death. War is necessary only as every other sin is necessary—because men choose to engage in it; and of all human woes there are none for which there is so little real occasion.

II. War is UNREASONABLE. The very fact that

it is unnecessary, proves it unreasonable; for nothing but the direst necessity can justify it, and make it consistent with reason and good sense.

God has endowed us with minds capable of thought and reflection, and designed to guide us in choosing between opposite courses of conduct. But where are these in war? What *reason* is there in mowing down whole ranks of humanity, for the sake of deciding questions with which physical force has nothing to do? What reason in draining all the resources of a nation in order to recover or protect a trifling sum; or in disgracing a nation with crime in order to resent a real or imagined insult; or in adjusting by brute force and low cunning those disputes which it is the prerogative of the mind to settle? What conduct can be more irrational than to make so proverbially fickle a thing as war a sole arbiter of right and wrong, and to submit the most complicated questions of state to the decision of a battle-field? Its most learned advocates have never attempted to prove that there is a necessary connection between might and right, or weakness and wrong. The strength of armies and the skill of generals do not depend upon the justness of the cause which calls them forth. As with individuals, a holy, upright man, with truth upon his side, may be "in bodily presence weak," while his adversary is a brutal ruffian of giant strength, so it may be with nations.

What a state of society that would be in which physical strength was the only arbiter of justice! Could we find a spot where men were so degraded, we should see the strong trampling upon the rights of the weak, feeble innocence outraged and crushed, and no truth or justice recognized except when connected with a brawny arm, or skill in the use of weapons. Upon witnessing these frequent triumphs of might over justice, we should almost be led to question whether God had endowed these beings with reason, and should conclude that they were more akin to the wild beasts, whose conduct they emulate, than to rational, intelligent men, whose form they wear. Such a picture is presented in every war, and such a scene is often enacted in the family of Christian nations.

It was once the custom to try cases of alleged guilt by subjecting the accused person to severe ordeals. He was required to lift a redhot iron in his hand, or to walk over heated ploughshares, or to plunge his arm in boiling water. If he was possessed of sufficient physical nerve to endure the test without flinching, he was declared innocent. If so feeble as to be easily overcome by it, no further proof of his guilt was deemed necessary. We are accustomed to smile at the superstitious simplicity of our ancestors, who gravely tried the most important offences by these ordeals, or by judicial combat; coming generations will, in like manner, wonder at us who try national offences, and redress national wrongs, by the equally unreasonable ordeal of *war*. There is scarcely more connection between justice and war, than between it and redhot ploughshares. Right and truth depend no more upon a victorious issue to the one, than innocence depended upon a triumphant endurance of the other. In both of them the only vindication of the right is the superiority of physical force or endurance.

If it were seriously proposed in our national councils to abolish all laws, and return to the practice of *trial by ordeal*, the suggestion would not only find no support, but would mark the person offering it as beside himself. How, then, should we regard those governments which, in plain disregard of reason's clearest dictates, persist in the practice of *trial by battle.* The absurdity is as great in the one instance as it would be in the other. Well will it be for the nations of the earth when they shall arise to the exercise of their nobler powers of mind, and devote to the amicable adjustment of their differences that *reason* which is now so generally employed to increase them; or rather, well will it be for them when Reason's rays, purified and strengthened by an enlightened Christianity, shall shed sweet beams upon that upward path which leads to the reign of *universal peace.*

III. War is UNJUST. Nothing is just which is not right and reasonable, and in accordance with the revealed will of God. War, as a system, is made up of the grossest *injustice* to all who are concerned in it. In instances of individual differences, the law affords to both parties the means of securing justice. In order to this, it provides for a trial by jury, or a reference to disinterested arbitrators. But how is it with nations? Each assumes the right to be its own judge and jury, to decide upon the question at issue, and to decree and inflict the penalty. Governments and sovereigns—themselves the parties most deeply interested, and their minds warped by prejudice and passion—arrogate the sole right to pronounce judgment upon those who offend them, and enforce their partial, one-sided decisions at the point of the sword. They allow no right or opportunity of trial by jury, and until quite recently have seldom permitted the mediation or arbitration of neutral powers. From their decisions there is no appeal, and the victims of their oppressive verdicts are compelled to fight as their only alternative. As has been already observed, justice is not necessarily secured by battles; and the poor culprits who are arraigned at the bar of war, must make muskets and bayonets their only plea, rest their defence upon the courage and skill of their soldiers, and look for their verdict of acquittal or condemnation in their victory or defeat. What a libel upon justice to have the contested point *fought* to its decision by the accuser and accused! Men long since discovered the injustice of this mode of trial among *individuals*. and abolished it. When will they perceive that it is equally unjust with *nations?*

Again, justice would seem to require that the punishment decreed fall only upon *the guilty.* In war, it seldom visits them, but descends with all its weight upon the innocent. Now has any government such a right to the lives of its subjects, that it can sacrifice them for the sake of punishing others? In war it is not the rulers who suffer. They, having decreed the mischief, sit aloof from it, and see their subjects, men who are but slightly interested in the contested question, if at all, hewn down by thousands. As the French troops were embarking for Constantinople, in 1853, an old man exclaimed mournfully, "There goes my only child, to fight for a cause he does not understand, and against men with whom he never had a difference." Now what justice is there in thus dragging a man from his peaceful pursuits and his rightful home, condemning him to toilsome marches, fatigue, disease, and immoral influences, and then bidding him stain his hands with the blood of those who have never injured either him or his country, and who have done nothing deserving of death? What justice in bidding him stain his *soul* with blackest crimes, and then expose his life to those who have no cause for hating him? What justice in desolating happy homes, bereaving fond hearts, and clothing half the land in mourning, in order to satisfy a mere caprice or avenge an insult? The evils of war fall almost wholly upon the people. By far the greater number of sufferers are those who are innocent of any wrong against their destroyers. Mark the course of an invading army. See the fields laid waste; the families ruined; the peaceful men and women and children made wretched or destroyed. *What have they done* to deserve such suffering? Look on the battle-field. How have those troops offended against one another, or what crimes has the one army committed against the government of the other? They are only the dupes and substitutes of the real offenders, if any there are; and while innocence is there becoming guilt, and pouring out the life's blood of both soul and body, the parties who impose their quarrels upon them are lounging in their comfortable homes, and smiling approvingly upon the self-sacrificing *patriotism* of their brave subjects.

Justice presides not over scenes of strife.

The turbulence of the battle-field is not his congenial element. If you look for him he is found only amid calm, peaceful scenes, where reason and judgment wield their quiet supremacy, and not a breath of passion disturbs the even balance of his scales. And Justice speaks not in the roar of artillery, and the ravings of frenzied blasphemy, but in tones of manly firmness and deep deliberation. *Injustice* of the most glaring kind rules every phase of war, from its first declaration to the last victim whom it leaves dead upon the field.

IV. War is INHUMAN. We need not rehearse its cruelties; the view of them which has already passed before us is sufficiently shocking. The humane mind instinctively recoils from the horrid barbarities of the battle-field. There are those who succeed, by dint of long habit, in accustoming themselves to behold such scenes unmoved; but they are themselves living monuments to the evils of a practice which can transform pitying, feeling men into such unnatural monsters. Were it not for the fact that war hardens its votaries to the view of suffering, and crushes all their tender sensibilities to an alarming degree, it would probably have ceased long ago for the want of hands to wage it. Viewing mankind in general, and not merely the practised soldier, whose trade is murder, war is a violent outrage upon human nature. It arouses the whole being of man in indignant revolt; and every emotion of love, kindness, pity, sympathy, humanity, and virtue unite in protesting against it, and overwhelming him who engages in it with shame and horror. He who for the first time fights an enemy in battle, must meanwhile contend resolutely against his own violated feelings and instincts. He may temporarily overcome them in the wild excitement and thirst for vengeance or glory which impel him forward, giving him no time to think or feel; but he must pass through a severe struggle, and make violent sacrifice of his humanity, before he can become "a good soldier." A letter-writer from the Crimea has thus described the feelings of a soldier in time of conflict: "Before the battle begins, it is usual to feel no little tremor, and many cheeks which are known to be in communication with stout hearts, blanch visibly. As the conflict becomes imminent, courage returns, and with the first flow of blood, an enthusiasm is raised which constantly increases, and very seldom flags in the least until the last shot is fired. *The effect of seeing a comrade shot down is generally to excite an unappeasable thirst for vengeance against the foe,* though in the end one 'gets used to it.'"

The following affecting statement is from a letter written by an English sailor to his wife, and describes his sensations upon killing a man for the first time. "We were ordered to fire. I took steady aim, and fired on my man at about sixty yards. He fell like a stone. At the same time a broadside from the —— went in among the trees, and the enemy disappeared, we could scarcely tell how. I felt as though I must go up to *him*, to see whether he was dead or alive. He lay quite still, and I was more afraid of him lying so, than when he stood facing me a few moments before. It's a strange feeling to come over you all at once that you have killed a man. He had unbuttoned his jacket, and was pressing his hand over the front of his chest, where the wound was. He breathed hard, and the blood poured from the wound and also from his mouth every breath he took. His face was white as death, and his eyes looked so big and bright as he turned them and stared at me—*I shall never forget it.* He was a fine young fellow, not more than five and twenty. I went down on my knees beside him, and my breast felt so full, as though my own heart would burst. He had a real English face, and did not look like an enemy. What I felt I never can tell, but if my life would have saved his, I believe I should have given it. I laid his head on my knee, and he tried to speak, but his voice was gone. I could not tell a word he said, and every time he tried to speak, the blood poured out so, I knew it would soon be over. I am not ashamed to say that I was worse than he, for he never shed a tear, and I couldn't help it. . . . . I was wondering how I could leave him to die, and no one near him, when he had something like a convulsion for a moment, and then his face rolled over, and with a sigh he was gone. I trust the Almighty has received his soul. I laid his head gently down on the grass, and left him. It seemed so strange when I looked at him for the last time—I somehow thought of every thing I had heard about the Turks and Russians, and the rest of them—but *all that seemed so far off, and the dead man so near.*"

V. War is INEFFICACIOUS. Whether there be any other means of redressing national wrongs or not, experience shows that *war does not*, in most cases, accomplish that end. Its chief efficacy is for the infliction of wrongs. It is a system which, while causing innumerable other evils, rarely affords relief from the ones that prompt it. As far as regards any positive good accruing from it, it is generally of no avail. God may sometimes overrule it for good, as he does the whirlwind, pestilence, and fire; those ends, however, which men design that it shall secure—unless they are the unworthy ones of retaliation and revenge—are seldom attained by it. It usually parts the combatants yet more widely asunder, and only casts new obstacles in the way of their amicable agreement.

Vattel, a writer of high authority, has said, "It is an error, no less absurd than pernicious, to say that war is to *decide* controversies between those who, as is the case with nations, acknowledge no judge. *It is power or prudence, rather than right, that victory usually declares for.*" Jefferson says, "War is an instrument *entirely inefficient towards redressing wrongs*, and multiplies, instead of indemnifying losses." "The wars of Europe for these two hundred years past," says an eminent English writer, "by the confession of all parties, have really ended in the advantage of none, but to the manifest detriment of all." As a general thing, it may be confidently asserted that war is *useless*. The curse of God is attached to it, and it bears none but bitter fruits. As this branch of our subject has been in part anticipated, we need not dwell upon it.

VI. War is INGLORIOUS. We read much of the splendor of martial achievements, of "brilliant victories," and "glorious conquests." Conquerors have been crowned with wreaths and garlands, and men have vied in doing them reverent homage. Heathen nations have even deified their most successful warriors—and have not Christian nations at times practically enthroned them above the Prince of peace? History has prostituted its pen to the work of transmitting their names with lustre to posterity, and has fatally dazzled many weak minds with the halo of glory which it has cast around them. All this, however, is a mere disguise, which cloaks from view the shameful reality.

It is time that the mask were stripped off from this horrid monster, and his true character revealed in all its hideous deformity. It is time that the nations ceased to glory in their shame, and to look for honor in that which only stains them with infamy. It is for Christians of the present day to unite in reversing the erroneous sentiments of mankind upon this subject, by no longer countenancing the falsehood that even the most successful war is *glorious.*

The divine word affords the only correct standard of national as well as individual greatness. It says, "*Righteousness exalteth a nation, but sin is a reproach to any people.*" Prov. 14 : 34. Nothing, then, is creditable which is not *right.* No degree of factitious splendor can impart a real glory to crime. Whatever be its form, and whatever its extenuating circumstances, it is in itself, and from its very nature, a disgrace. How inglorious, then, must that practice be which involves the commission of so many crimes against God and man. Were not our minds warped by the world's false maxims, we should regard the nation that unjustly engages in it as branded with deepest ignominy.

We should see that to wage war is, in most cases, a far greater degradation than to be defeated in it; and that they who resort to it in order to humble an enemy, thereby lower themselves to a depth yet more humiliating. There is no disgrace in being wronged and oppressed—and if it be in a good cause, and patiently endured and forgiven, there is glory in it; but there is disgrace in wronging and oppressing others.

If we look at war as it really is, and divested of its disguises, we shall see that it is usually made up of those courses of conduct on the part of nations which are considered infamous when practised by individuals. Is it glorious to rob or wantonly destroy another's property? or to engage in prize-fighting? or to attack defenceless persons, and triumph over women and children? or to take advantage of another's insecurity, and like the midnight assassin, murder a victim when he is off his guard? or to sacrifice other persons in order to screen ourselves from injury? Such actions, when performed by individuals, are universally pronounced dishonorable. Why are they not held to be equally base when done by *nations?* They are in reality far more so, if there is any proportion between the extent of a disgraceful action and the degree of shame that attaches to it. Well asks the poet,

"Is death more cruel from a private dagger,
Than in a field from murdering swords of thousands?
Or does the number slain make slaughter glorious?"

The truth is, that even when war is necessary and unavoidable, it should be viewed as a most humiliating alternative. The successful general, or the one who has succeeded in murdering the greatest number, instead of being applauded and worshipped as a demigod, should be greatly commiserated. The soldiers, instead of being distinguished by their gay uniforms, should carefully avoid making known their real profession; and the epaulet should be regarded as discreditable to its wearer. Every battle, whether victorious or otherwise, should cause each patriot cheek to burn with shame; and should be announced, not by booming cannon and pealing bells, but by flags at half-mast and tolling bells, in token of the national dishonor. Thus war should be regarded even in those rare cases when it may be necessary. *If it were thus regarded, it would soon be discovered that it is far from necessary.* Such a state of public sentiment would be enough to overturn every plea in its favor, and there would then be no lack of expedients which should settle the difficulties of nations, and yet spare them this mutual infamy.

It cannot be questioned that the false halo of glory which is thrown by most poets and historians about successful warfare, whether right or wrong, has done much towards perpetuating this disgraceful practice. Our literature is debased with many glowing accounts of military achievements, which exert a most pernicious influence in favor of war. Such representations captivate and poison many a youthful mind, excite false notions of honor, and lead men to admire and practise those courses of conduct which God abhors, and the Bible condemns. Poetry, painting, and eloquence have vied in honoring the destroyers of mankind; and to them we are to a great measure indebted for the military spirit which so widely prevails. Alas, that genius should thus pervert its sacred trust, and maintain an unholy alliance with sin and shame! Well will it be for the world when all our popular literature, and the voice of public opinion shall be made to subserve the cause of righteousness and true honor.

A most important step will have been gained when the public is led to view this subject in its true light. We ask all Christians and philanthropists to do their part towards bringing about so desirable a change. Let the heroes of war be plucked from their lofty pedestals, and let the places in the world's esteem, which most of them have so unworthily occupied, be filled by those who are truly glorious—the meek, the loving, and the forgiving. Let the laurels which have so long crowned the brows of Cæsar, Alexander, and Napoleon, encircle those of Stephen and John, and all martyrs to peace. Above all, let the forgiving *Jesus* be so enthroned in every land and in every heart, that he shall be looked upon as the true type of national and individual grandeur. Let the truth be everywhere inculcated, that it is more glorious to suffer wrong than to do wrong—that it is glorious to forbear, but inglorious to resent—glorious to cultivate the arts of peace, but inglorious to foster those of war—glorious to obey God, but inglorious to obey passion—

glorious to do right, but inglorious to do wrong—that "righteousness exalteth a nation, but sin is a reproach to any people."

The church and many in the world have learned to attach the idea of true glory to the *millennium*. Prophecy has given us an insight into the nature of that glory, and one important feature of it is summed up in the words, "*They shall not learn war any more.*" The promise is richly suggestive. It teaches us that the splendors of Messiah's reign are not to be those of brilliant victories and martial renown, but such as can only exist in the absence of these, and in the universal prevalence of peace. The Christian mind will require no stronger evidence that war is inglorious. The Christian nation need require no other, and will best promote its true dignity and grandeur by conforming, not to the false human standards of the past, but to that divine one which looms up from the millennial future.

CHAPTER XII.

WAR TESTED BY THE GOSPEL, OR WAR UNCHRISTIAN.

If, as has been shown, the *Right Way* prescribed in the gospel is applicable to nations, and rulers are under solemn obligations to conform to it, it requires no extended argument to prove that *war is, in general,* UNCHRISTIAN.

I. *War is a violation of* THE LAW OF LOVE. See Matt. 22 : 39 ; 5 : 44.

It is a system which is both the offspring and parent of hate. We cannot conceive of a nation's loving its neighbor as itself, and yet inflicting upon it those injuries which it is the avowed object of war to produce. More especially it is impossible to conceive of war in connection with an obedience to the precept, "*Love your enemies.*" It is generally considered a sufficient reason for this practice that one government or one nation has assumed the attitude of hostility towards another. However the public may deprecate such an abuse of friendly relations as the invasion of an unoffending country, there seems to have been, with the masses, but one opinion as to the justness of punishing by battle those who have injured us. If a ruler or government, when bent upon war, can but make it appear that any particular nation is "the enemy," the desired end is easily gained. That magic word usually suffices to arouse the public indignation, to open the floodgates of passion, to enkindle a false patriotism, to unlock the national resources, and to make the deluded people the willing tools of scheming and ambitious politicians. Every consideration of duty, honor, interest, and right is at once overwhelmed. The fact that a tribe or nation either has committed or designs committing a hostile act, is deemed a sufficient excuse for assailing its commerce, and at any cost crippling its energies and destroying its lives. The practical maxim of most governments appears to be even more selfish and unloving than that of the heartless pharisaic Jews. Without fully admitting the first half of their precept, "Thou shalt love thy neighbor," excepting when it appears to be for their interest to do so, they adopt in its fullest extent the second, Thou shalt "hate thine enemy."

If the gospel be the only rule of right, the spirit and conduct required of nations is the precise opposite of this. Its precepts demand that we do nothing to a hostile power which is not consistent with, and prompted by a hearty love towards it. The injurious conduct of enemies should be met with kind forbearance, and a tender regard for their interests. The inquiry should be, not how we may best retaliate, but how we may do them the most good. The national enthusiasm should be aroused, not to the work of hating, but to that of loving and blessing them. Even should the display of this spirit fail to overcome their hostility—a failure which it is probable would seldom if ever occur—and should self-defence demand that some degree of resistance be opposed to them, it would still be our duty, as far as possible, to love them, and to refrain from injuring them to any greater degree than necessity required. Such is clearly the nation's duty, as set forth in the precept, "Love your enemies."

But how widely opposite are the law of love, and the generally accepted law of nations! Where is love in those councils which deliberately plot the ruin of a foreign power? Ah, it is studiously banished from such assemblies; and it is too generally the case that only ambition, envy, hatred, and revenge find entrance there. Who will say that a ruler loves that nation which he bids his armies do their utmost to destroy? Where is love in the nation's heart, when it is draining its resources and risking its lives for the sake of avenging itself upon another nation; when the universal desire to crush an offending power pervades the masses of the people, and even, too often in awful mockery, has its place in their prayers; and when they celebrate with festivals and Te Deums each new triumph of cruelty over large numbers of their fellow-men? Where is love in the battle-field? Does its soft voice speak in the roar of artillery, or the strains of martial music, or the raving curses of the imbruted soldiery? Does love aim the fatal shot, and direct the bayonet to human hearts? Does love wound and maim and kill intelligent creatures of God, and hurl undying souls into perdition? No: for "love worketh no ill to his neighbor."

II. War is a violation of those precepts of the gospel which require FORGIVENESS. See

Matt. 6 : 12, 14, 15 ; Mark 11 : 25 ; Luke 17 : 3, 4 ; Col. 3 : 12, 13 ; Eph. 4 : 31, 32.

Frequent opportunities for the exercise of this virtue are afforded in the career of every nation, yet how rarely it is exhibited. Even when an injury is not violently resented, how few think of forgiving it. If, for reasons of state policy, it is allowed to go unpunished, it still excites hatred and rancor in the public mind, and kindles a flame which is liable, upon the slightest occasion, to burst forth in all the desolating fury of war. To withhold chastisement from an offending nation, when it is in our power to inflict it, is deemed magnanimous. To *forgive* its injurious conduct is such a moral triumph as has been seldom, if ever achieved. Even when outward peace is maintained, the offending power is still viewed with resentment; and the trespass which is not "redressed," or wiped away with blood, is generally permitted to rankle for years, until time, and not duty, has buried it in oblivion.

That war is opposed to the exercise of forgiveness, need hardly be said. The two are as widely different as can well be imagined, and none will assert that they are otherwise. The whole practice is an exhibition, upon a grand scale, of an unforgiving spirit. It is such in its origin, in its entire conduct, in the dispositions which it requires and fosters, and in its invariable results. This fact is too plain to require comment.

Such being the case, what a fearful curse must rest upon every unforgiving nation. For all the awful threatenings uttered against those who cherish this spirit, are applicable to nations, as to individuals. History has proved that God, in his providential dealings with our race, treats every nation or government as an accountable moral person—there being, however, this difference between them and individuals, that as nations exist, in their peculiar character, only in this world, their punishment must of necessity be inflicted here, while that of individuals is more often reserved for the world to come. A knowledge of this fact will afford the reason of many national reverses which seem otherwise unaccountable. They are often the fulfilment of that divine threat which has so long been sounded in the ears of man, "If ye forgive not men their trespasses, neither will your Father forgive your trespasses." Matt. 6:15. Every country sins often and grievously against God, and has much need of his forgiveness; but although it is implored in thousands of sanctuaries, and special days are set apart for the purpose of humiliation and prayer, the nation that engages unjustly in war forfeits all claim to it. Its guilt is likely to remain unpardoned, and it continues exposed to the full weight of its deserved punishment, and must expect at some time to be overtaken by it. We commend this thought to the attention of rulers, and ask whether they are willing, by disobeying the gospel, to bring upon the nation the retribution of its guilt, and oppose a barrier to the prayers of pious citizens or subjects. Will they not much better secure their country's prosperity, and avert the dangers with which its sins may threaten it, by heeding the promise, "If ye forgive men their trespasses, your heavenly Father will also forgive you," and by enabling the prayer to go up consistently in the nation's behalf, from thousands of loving and patriot hearts, "Forgive us our debts, *as we forgive our debtors?*"

III. War is a violation of the precept, "RE-

SIST NOT EVIL." See Matt. 5 : 39 ; 1 Pet. 3 : 9 ; Rom. 12 : 14, 21.

Applying to this branch of our subject the rules laid down in our Lord's sermon on the mount, we find that it is a nation's duty to suffer most kinds of wrong, rather than resist them. War, however, is a mutual infliction of and resistance to injury. Its guilt, too, is aggravated by the fact that the resistance which it makes is of so severe and bloody a character. How fearfully criminal those nations must be in the sight of God, who not only disobey this precept, but, in their violation of it, inflict such enormous evils. For instance, when the offence resisted is the comparatively trivial one of a national insult, or a slight injury to commerce, how grossly sinful is that resistance which destroys millions of property upon both sides, and many valuable lives, and entails upon the two nations all the evils of a state of war! Unchristian as it is for one or a few persons to resent and wrongfully resist injuries, the crime becomes of a tenfold magnitude when *nations* are guilty of it.

IV. War is yet more plainly a violation of those precepts which require us to RENDER

GOOD FOR EVIL. See Matt. 5 : 44, 45 ; 1 Pet. 3 : 9 ; Rom. 12 : 14, 17, 20, 21.

These precepts would seem to demand that nations not only endure ordinary wrongs without resistance, but that they also confer positive good upon those who offend them. Thus, in cases of injury received, the *right way* of responding to it would often be by an effort to benefit the hostile country. Instead of a declaration of war, there should be proofs of continued amity. Instead of studying its weak points in order to attack them, we should study its wants in order to relieve them. Instead of prayers for the destruction of the enemy, there should be prayers for their forgiveness, and best temporal and spiritual welfare. Such a course might also be urged as likely to afford the best defence against a hostile power, and as tending to disarm aggression.

That the practice of war is any other than a violation of this duty, none will venture to assert. So far from even permitting an obedience to the precept, "If thine enemy hunger, feed him ; if he thirst, give him drink," it denounces and shoots as traitors those who are detected in giving "aid and comfort" to the enemy. It is hardly possible to conceive of a more palpable violation of this duty than is afforded in *sieges*, where hunger and thirst are often made the chief weapons for the subduing of cities.

V. War is a direct violation of the golden rule, "ALL THINGS WHATSOEVER YE WOULD THAT MEN SHOULD DO TO YOU, DO YE EVEN SO TO THEM." Matt. 7 : 12.

So thoroughly has the principle of selfishness become inwoven with almost all national intercourse, that this obligation has seldom, if ever, been recognized by governments. Yet it is the summary of national as well as individual duty. We need not pause to prove that the war system is as utterly at variance with the conduct here required, as it is with the spirit of the parallel precept, "Thou shalt love thy neighbor as thyself." The fact is so plain that probably none will deny it.

With regard to all these precepts, it is perhaps sufficient to have shown that they are applicable to nations. This fact being once admitted, the intelligent reader will perceive at a glance that war in general is inconsistent with the requirements of the gospel, and that a war spirit is precisely the opposite of a Christian spirit.

Let us contrast them. Compare the demands of war, as most commonly originated and prosecuted, with those of Christianity. *Christ* says, "Blessed are the poor in spirit," "the meek," "the merciful," "the peacemakers," and the "persecuted for righteousness' sake." *War* says, "Blessed are the proud in spirit, the resentful, the unmerciful, the warlike, and those who revenge themselves upon their revilers and persecutors." *Christ* says, "Whosoever is angry with his brother without a cause, shall be in danger of the judgment." *War* says, "Whosoever cherishes not anger against those whom his rulers bid him hate, is a traitor and a coward." *Christ* says, "Resist not evil;" "Love your enemies, bless them that curse you, do good unto them that hate you, and pray for them which despitefully use you, and persecute you, that ye may be the children of your Father which is in heaven." *War* says, "Resist evil with yet greater evil, hate and kill your enemies, curse and pray *against* them that curse and persecute you, that ye may be patriotic subjects." *Christ* says, "All things whatsoever ye would that men should do to you, do ye even so to them." *War* says, "All evil things which men do to you, recompense them with a tenfold evil." The whole spirit of Christianity inculcates the duty of love; that of war requires hatred. The one demands the exercise of kindness, forbearance, and forgiveness; the other insists upon cruelty, resentment, and revenge. The one requires purity of heart and life; the other stains both with crime. The one saves souls; the other destroys them. The one fits men for heaven; the other for hell. The one looks forward to a reign of peace; the other throws obstacles in its way, and perpetuates enmity and war. *The one is from God; the other from the devil.*

War then is, in general, *unchristian.* It is, as we have seen, unnecessary, unreasonable, unjust, inhuman, inefficacious, and inglorious; but its worst feature is this, that it is unchristian. And if such be its character, is it not one of the most stupendous iniquities in which men can engage? If an evil and a crime, it is an enormous evil, and a glaring crime. Involving as it does such tremendous interests, its good or bad results must be of proportionate importance. As its results are in most cases *only evil*, how vast must be that evil! No human mind can fathom it—only the eye of God can behold it in all its length and breadth. Yet the view of it which arrests our gaze reveals enough of its enormity to make it stand out as, comparatively, the greatest sin and direst curse that has ever infested the world.

CHAPTER XIII.

THE SUBSTITUTE FOR WAR—ARBITRATION.

It has, we think, been shown that war is in general the *wrong way* of adjusting national differences. Whether there be any other mode of securing the ends proposed by it or not, this one is clearly condemned by both reason and revelation. If, then, there were no good substitute for it, and the nations must either suffer wrong or fight, it would seem as if they should in most instances embrace the suffering as the better alternative. Whether the remedy which we shall now propose be adequate or not, we must still insist that war, as a system, ought to be none the less speedily and decisively *abolished.*

To suppose, however, that there is no remedy for it, would be as derogatory to reason and common-sense as to the moral government of God. *It should be taken for granted,* until experience has proved to the contrary, that there is a better way of solving national difficulties—a way more consistent with our character as reasonable beings, and with our duties to one another and to God. Where the right spirit existed, men would not be long in discovering this *Right Way;* and means would soon be found which should harmonize the practice of mutual justice with that of mutual love, and apply to the intercourse of nations that gospel which so happily regulates the intercourse of individuals. The necessity of such a means has long been felt by Christians and philanthropists. Franklin says, "We daily make great improvements in natural philosophy; there is one I wish to see in morals—the discovery of a plan that would induce and oblige nations to settle their disputes without first cutting one another's throats. When will human reason be sufficiently improved to see the advantage of this?"

Where shall such a plan be found? The parallel already drawn between individuals and nations suggests a few valuable hints upon this subject. A man who deems himself injured rarely resorts to physical violence for redress, but submits his grievances to a jury of his peers, who endeavor to decide upon them with reference to right and justice. *Why may not nations do the same?* Is not the very existence of laws in civilized communities a standing rebuke to the lawless violence of nations, and a proof that their differences may be adjusted in a far more righteous manner than by an appeal to arms? Our courts of justice accomplish for individuals the ends that are professedly aimed at by nations in war. They therefore point out a simple and obvious substitute for war, which the nations would do well to adopt. For what is there to prevent the reference of their difficulties to *a jury of nations*, through their representatives, who shall pronounce upon them an impartial judgment? Whether such jury consist of one, two, or three, chosen by the parties themselves, or of a perpetual court instituted for the purpose, it would assuredly secure the ends of justice to a far greater degree than *trial by battle.*

We would urge as the most simple, and in the present state of public opinion, most practicable substitute for war, ARBITRATION. By this we mean the submitting of national difficulties to the judgment and decision of one or more arbitrators, or umpires, to be chosen by the parties at variance, and the including of an article to that effect in their treaties with one another.

This plan would not in any way interfere with well-timed efforts at *negotiation.* Indeed, that step should always be resorted to in the first instance, as being the best calculated, when successful, to satisfy both parties. The fact that the next and *final* remedy is arbitration, and that war is entirely out of the question, will greatly assist their efforts at a mutual agreement. When, however, this first and most natural means has failed, let the two parties feel themselves bound by a solemn written obligation, *to submit their case to the judgment of one or more friendly powers, and to abide by their verdict as a final one.*

This is no new mode of adjusting differences, but has often been practised by individuals, and occasionally by nations. It is frequently resorted to by wise and Christian men, as preferable even to the regular course of law, because avoiding not only much trouble and expense, but also much of that bitterness of feeling which is too often engendered by litigation. Its principle is the same with that of trial by jury—only differing from it in this respect, that it allows to the parties employing it the privilege of choosing their own arbitrators. Every trial in our courts of justice is a reference of a disputed question to umpires chosen by society. The propriety of such a reference is evident. It is founded upon the just supposition that no man is qualified to judge in a case in which his own interests are at stake; and that none but those whose minds are disinterested and unbiased, are competent to award to it a righteous decision. *This principle is equally applicable to nations.* Rulers and governments are also incapable of rightly adjudicating their own controversies. The same reasons, therefore, which demand opportunities for reference or legal process in a community of subjects, also require it in the community of governments. If, as has been proved from the highest authorities, nations ought to be "regarded as moral persons," and as "under the same obligations that are binding upon individuals," then it is plainly their duty to adjust their disputes in a way similar to that employed by individuals.

In commendation of this plan, we may quote from the acknowledged masters of international law. *Grotius*, its founder, says, "War should never be declared until all other means of redress have been faithfully tried." *Vattel* says, "Nature gives us no right to have recourse to force, but where mild and pacific methods are ineffectual. When sovereigns cannot agree about their pretensions, they sometimes trust the decision of their disputes to arbitrators. This method is very reasonable, and very conformable to the law of nature in determining differences that do not directly interest the safety of the nation. *Though the strict right may be mistaken by the arbitrators, it is still more to be feared that it will be overwhelmed by the fate of arms.*"

This practice has often been resorted to by nations with signal success. The kings of Denmark and Sweden formerly bound themselves by treaty to refer to one another the differences which might arise between them and their respective senates. "The princes of Neufchatel," says Vattel, "established in 1406 the canton of Berne the judge and perpetual arbitrator of their disputes. The Swiss have had the precaution, in all their alliances among themselves, and even in those they have contracted with the neighboring powers, to agree beforehand on the manner in which their disputes were to be submitted to arbitrators, in case they could not themselves adjust them in an amicable manner. This wise precaution has not a little contributed to maintain the Helvetic republic in that flourishing state which secures its liberty, and renders it respectable throughout Europe." France and Mexico had recourse to this expedient in their treaty of peace in 1839. Instead of enforcing their respective claims for alleged injuries, they mutually agreed to refer them to the arbitrament of a third power. The leading cabinets of Europe have, of late years, employed it with much success. Our own government has referred three of its disputes to as many European sovereigns. A question relating to the interpretation of our last treaty of peace with Great Britain was referred to the emperor of Russia; that concerning our North-eastern boundary, to the king of the Netherlands; and certain difficulties with Mexico, to the king of Prussia. Having been successful upon almost every occasion, this plan is now regarded with much favor by civilized nations; and it seems only requisite that it be formally incorporated in all national treaties, in order to secure its universal adoption.

We urge its *incorporation in articles of treaty*, because it is only by such means that it can be made obligatory, and become an established system. Any substitute for war, in order to be successful, must be agreed upon, and made a matter of solemn, deliberate compact in time of peace. Nations, like individuals, are not in a fit condition to see clearly and select the right, when their passions are aroused by controversy; and it is therefore not safe to rely upon their *then* resorting to a means of reconciliation, to which, in hours of calmness and kind feeling, they might willingly pledge themselves. Such an article as we recommend would anticipate whatever difficulties might afterwards occur, and provide beforehand for their amicable settlement.

To this plan there can be opposed no reasonable objection, while there is much that can be said in its favor. The difficulty may occur to some minds that the treaty might be violated, and that there is then no force to compel its fulfilment. We reply, all other treaties are equally liable to be broken, but is that fact deemed a sufficient reason for not forming them? While, however, the abolition of war might seem to take away the means of enforcing this compact, there would yet remain a power mightier than resides in any army—that of *public opinion*. This is a force which is often overlooked, yet one that is possessed of an almost irresistible, and growing efficacy. The common sentiment of the people, having been at first manifested in demanding this pledge of peace, would also make itself heard and obeyed in the work of maintaining it inviolate. The nation that should so break its plighted faith as not to fulfil and abide by such a contract, would probably be branded with ignominy, and made a mark for the scorn and contempt of every other nation. Besides, if this plan should once be generally adopted, the blessings of peace would be too highly appreciated by the masses of the people to allow of their being lightly perilled; and every government would feel itself interested in punishing in some peaceful, yet effective manner, the nation that should dare violate this principle of *international law*.

If, however, for any reason not yet discernible, this plan should prove unsuccessful, those animated by the proper spirit might devise some other mode which should accomplish so desirable an object. The formation of a congress of nations, or a perpetual court, composed of representatives from every government, has been proposed and ably advocated. The prevalence of right feelings throughout Christendom would render this plan a feasible one, and secure to every aggrieved nation the privilege of an impartial trial upon principles of law and equity. Surely one or the other of these means, or both united, or some other yet to be devised, can be adopted as the *Right Way* of conducting the intercourse of nations.

The advantages of some such course over the one commonly resorted to, are obvious. It would secure the administration of a far higher degree of justice than is gained by war, and probably as high a degree as can be attained among men. It would prevent those gross oppressions which are so often practised by strong nations. It would afford a security to the defenceless, and guarantee them such a redress for injuries as could be obtained by no other means. It would maintain the independence of nations, by affording a check to ambitious schemes of conquest and aggrandizement. It would substitute reason for passion, kindness for cruelty, courtesy and honorable consideration for ruffian brutality and bloody violence, the supremacy of mind for that of physical force, and of right for wrong. It would, in averting war, avert many of the direst evils that have afflicted mankind, and in securing perpetual peace, secure a perpetual train of blessings.

In bringing about these desirable results, *some nation must take the lead.* So vast a change as the one proposed cannot be accomplished in a day, nor by a simultaneous effort throughout Christendom. As in every other great reform, so in this, some one must dare to be singular, and stand boldly forth as its advocate. Every circumstance points to *America* as the best qualified to take the initiatory step in this grand work. Powerful and respected, her strength and influence would command the attention of the world towards any course upon which she might enter. Possessed of ample territories and immeasurable resources, she has nothing to gain, and every thing to lose by war. Exempted by her position from hostile attacks, she would incur no apparent risk by setting the example of a peaceful policy. A "model republic," she may, by spurning the control of the tyrant war, become a model of the most complete civil freedom. A nation eminently Christian, both consistency and the voice of public sentiment demand that she prove her high Christian character by conforming to the precepts of Jesus. May we not hope that among the providential designs of which she is to be the honored instrument, this one has its place; and that to her it may be given first to sound abroad the call that shall summon all nations to the approaching brotherhood of man?

Honored indeed will be that government to which this signal privilege shall be assigned. No nation has yet attained such a height of grandeur as will attach to that one which shall be the first to propose and carry out a plan for the abolition of war. The time is coming—and the present state of public opinion indicates that it may not be far distant—when that nation shall be esteemed the most glorious, which has dared to go forth as pioneer in the path of universal peace. It will receive the plaudits of men and angels, and its name will be repeated with joy and gratitude by coming generations. To have been the first to propose and effectually carry out a scheme for staying the effusion of human blood, will be a far higher honor to any land than for an individual to have discovered a continent, first floated a steam-boat, or made the lightning subservient to human agency. Upon such a nation will be breathed the heavenly benediction, "*Blessed are the peacemakers; for they shall be called the children of God.*"

Those rulers who are far-sighted, and who note the signs of the times and the promises of God's word, should hasten to secure this honor and this blessing; and the only strife among them should be, which shall stand foremost as the champion of humanity, and first enroll his name on that new scroll of renown which is to be written, not with tears and blood, but with the finger of truth and love. Those patriots who best love their country, and desire its lasting honor and prosperity, should vie in holy emulation to secure for it this true glory, and thus invoke in its behalf the blessings of God and men.

CHAPTER XIV.

THE BLESSINGS OF PEACE—THE MEANS OF SECURING IT.

In advocating the importance of peace, we would add to the consideration of duty, already urged, that of interest. Let us contemplate some of its more prominent blessings, and behold in each of them a powerful motive for securing it. We have seen a dim outline of the evils of war; and the view of its monstrous horrors has thrilled us with grief and indignation. As we now look upon the opposite picture, let its lovely attractions win upon our hearts, and inspire glowing desires for its full and permanent realization.

Contrast some of the principal features of each. Is war an incalculable *waste of property?* In peace the resources of the nation are allowed to flow in their legitimate and healthful channels; public and private enterprise is permitted the widest scope of operation; and capital remains undiverted from its proper spheres.

Men are not then drawn from fields of labor to those of battle; but the strong arms which in war must grasp the musket, wield in peace the hammer and the plough, and contribute to the common prosperity. The energy of business is unimpeded; wealth is accumulated; employment is furnished for all, and the nation is comparatively prosperous. Then, too, beneficence abounds. Much of the money which, in war, would have been worse than wasted, is in peace bestowed upon the needy and the wretched. Instead of being used for the infliction of suffering and death, it goes to relieve and cheer the sons of want. New plans of philanthropic benevolence are devised and carried out; the schemes of Christian enterprise are sustained; Bibles and tracts are circulated; the cause of missions is aided and carried forward, and every other effort for the world's evangelization meets with a hearty and liberal support. The experience of the thirty-nine years of general peace between the years 1815 and 1854, affords a striking exhibition of this fact. During that period, most of the benevolent societies which are the pride and glory of Britain and America were established; and their constant and increasing success is a signal proof of the blessings of peace in this respect.

Does war produce a disastrous *wreck of virtue and morality?* Peace, on the contrary, is highly favorable to them both. It not only avoids that deluge of vice and crime which floods a warring nation, but it is an important auxiliary to the growth of vital piety. Being itself an indispensable fruit of pure Christianity, it aids greatly in the cultivation of all its other fruits. Then Sabbaths are more honored, and sanctuaries more thronged; the "church-going bell" is oftener heard and heeded; and the voice of prayer and praise goes up from calm, peaceful hearts with greater fervor, and a greater likelihood of the divine acceptance. The nation being, in this respect at least, in the path of religious duty, its subjects may the more hopefully toil and pray for men's conversion. The whole system of the divine government assures us that it is at such times, if ever, that God will largely pour out his Spirit upon the churches. When we say that the revival of religion and the salvation of souls are among the blessings that pertain peculiarly to a state of peace, do we not say enough to enlist the sympathies and prayers and labors of all Christians in the work of securing it, and rendering it *permanent?*

Is war the *destruction of much domestic happiness*—the rending of many precious ties? Peace, on the contrary, preserves and augments the joys of every happy home. Like a guardian spirit, it presides over the humble cot and the lordly mansion, and permits no rude call of martial authority to summon its beloved inmates to destruction. The pure delights of the domestic hearth are invaded by no brutal sundering of fond connections; and no murderous whims of tyrants are allowed to fill the homes of the land with widowhood and orphanage. The pride and strength of the family circle toils cheerily on in his round of pleasant labor; and whatever else may cast a shadow on his heart, he feels that his country is the protection and defence of his elevated joys, and not their destruction; and that his patriotism does not require him to become a traitor to himself and those dependent upon him.

In like manner, peace is a guardian of every thing that constitutes a happy nation. It is to a great degree the security of its blessings, and the pledge of their continuance. There is hardly any interest of either governments or individuals to which it is not a necessary safeguard. Various and conflicting as they may be, they alike depend upon this for their protection. It is like one of those great walls which surrounded ancient cities. However different may have been the interests of the inhabitants, all felt that they would be put in peril if that bulwark were cast down. Thus peace engirdles the nation; and however various and even opposite may be the interests of its citizens, they would alike be made insecure the moment this wall of defence should fail them.

How beautiful, then, the spectacle presented by that land which is habitually at peace with all the world! See the thriving cities, towns, and villages, in which the hum of business, the clanking of manufactures, and the familiar sights and sounds of successful industry everywhere prevail. See the fields waving with the rich products of the soil—the garners teeming bountifully with food for man and beast—the harbors crowded with vessels, which bring their tributes of wealth and comfort from every land—

the smiling homes and firesides—the farmer singing at his plough, and the mechanic at his work. See the pervading life and energy which infuses itself into every department of human effort—the arts and sciences flourishing—education more and more widely extended—men running to and fro, and knowledge increased—the sphere of Christian activity enlarged—new churches built—missions and Sabbath-schools planted in destitute places—preachers and colporteurs sent forth to possess the land for Christ—the gospel acquiring daily new trophies to its divine power, and truth achieving new victories over error. Souls which might have been hardened and destroyed by the influences of war, are, under the mild reign of peace, rendered susceptible to the appeals of the pulpit and press, and instead of swelling the number of God's enemies, go to augment the army of his followers. Many a prodigal returns to his Father's house, and many a lost one is found. The church rejoices in an increase of her strength, and there is "joy in heaven among the angels of God" over repenting sinners. The heavenly hope finds readier access to human hearts—souls are saved, and God is glorified.

Nor is this all. The abounding life and exuberant sympathy of God's people will not, in time of peace, be confined to the narrow limits of a country or a continent, but overflow all boundaries, and baptize distant nations with the waters of life. As war impedes our efforts for the spread of the gospel, so peace encourages them, and enables the church to extend the circling ripples of her influence far and wide, until they embrace the globe itself. Peace places in our hands the means; peace affords opportunities for employing them to advantage; peace wafts the missionary across the seas; peace casts down the walls of prejudice, and secures a ready access to the homes and hearts of the heathen; peace sustains him there, and provides the bread of life for millions of famishing souls, and with the Bibles which it prints, affords a practical and convincing commentary upon its truths; peace affords the sinews which God strengthens for the demolition of Satan's kingdom; peace supplies, sustains, and coöperates with many of those forces which, under God, are to evangelize the world, and inaugurate the reign of the *Prince of peace.*

We do not affirm that the universal prevalence of peace would, of itself alone, secure all these blessings. No, "the word of God only, the grace of Christ only, the work of the Spirit only," are the hope of the nation, the church, and the world. Yet the very letter of that word, the character of that grace, and the known operations of that Spirit, assure us that if ever these blessings are to be looked for, it is in times of peace; and that, other things being equal, the reign of peace will go far towards securing the reign of happiness and righteousness.

"But how," it may be asked, "is peace to be rendered permanent? Acknowledging, as every reasonable mind must, its value, and the importance of retaining it, what can we do towards securing so desirable an object? We believe that peace shall prevail in the earth, but it is to be in the coming millennium. Then *God* will cause wars to cease, but *we* cannot accomplish so stupendous a change."

It is probably to the prevalence of this view of the subject that we must attribute much of the present lethargy in regard to it. Many Christians are appalled by the very magnitude of this blessing, and lose sight of their duty in the difficulties which seemingly attend it. Upon this principle, however, we might sit with folded hands and put forth no effort for the good of men. With at least equal justice we might say, "God only can convert souls, and we will therefore cease to labor for that end. Idolatry will not be wholly abolished until the millennium; of what avail are all our efforts against it?" Happily, however, Christians do not reason thus upon most other subjects. They generally acknowledge that the divine promises are to be fulfilled by *the divine blessing upon human effort.* This view is a correct one, and is proved true by experience. The cause of missions was undertaken, and is now prosecuted, under this belief; and its extraordinary success, when contrasted with the comparatively feeble efforts yet put forth, attests the power of Christian effort, when exerted wisely, and in conformity to the divine precepts and promises. It was thus that the gospel was first published in the earth; it was thus that the church was revived in the sixteenth century; and it is thus that the last great revival of God's work, in which he shall pour out his Spirit upon all flesh, is to be introduced.

In 1783 six humble and obscure, yet noble men, without political influence, but possessed of earnest philanthropy and strong faith in God, met in London to devise means for abolishing the *African slave-trade*. As the result of the agencies commenced by them, that infamous traffic was, twenty-four years afterwards, abolished by Great Britain, and is at this day forbidden by every Christian nation. Many of the readers of this volume can recollect when *intemperance* raged, a moral plague, throughout our country and the world. A small band of men, moved with love and pity for their race, put forth their hands to stay the curse. By God's blessing upon their *special efforts*, results have been gained of which it is probable that the most hopeful of them never dreamed. Temperance societies have sprung up in swift succession in every section of our country, and in many parts of Europe, while that cause has become the subject of legislation in several of our states; and there can be no doubt that many thousands of our fellow-beings have been rescued from this degrading vice in consequence of *the labors of a few earnest men, wisely directed towards this specific object.*

It is by similar means that war is to be abolished. We have no reason to believe that it will be removed by a miracle, or by any other than ordinary human instrumentalities. There is, on the contrary, every reason to believe that God will honor his church with the privilege of bringing about this, as well as every other triumph of the gospel. Indeed, he has already employed the peace societies of Great Britain and America in accomplishing much towards that triumph. In testimony of this, we may refer to one of America's ablest statesmen, *John Quincy Adams*, who publicly ascribed our escape from war with Mexico, in 1838, to the efforts of peace societies. We are warranted in the conviction that a yet larger blessing awaits them in the future. All that is required is earnest, judicious, prayerful, united *effort*, and the work will be done. Let the church enter upon it with that zeal which has characterized her Bible, tract, and missionary enterprises, and success is certain. Let her become one vast peace society; and let all denominations of evangelical Christians unite upon this subject, as upon a common platform, and make this cause one of those delightful ties by which they are fast becoming joined in the spirit of Christ. It will be to all a most desirable union, for what can tend more powerfully to the cessation of their often bitter and unprofitable controversies, than a common effort towards abolishing strife among others? Will they not, in promoting the peace of nations, best foster it among themselves, and find in their labors a fulfilment of the promise, "He that watereth, shall be watered also himself?"

The *kind* of effort to be employed, is readily suggested by the experience of every successful moral and religious enterprise. The means are at hand, and it only remains that they be diligently improved. First of all, let every pious heart aim at becoming itself thoroughly imbued with the principles of the gospel. Let Christians reflect upon the duty of maintaining both national and individual peace; and at the same time let them cherish the confident expectation, warranted by the word of prophecy, that *peace shall prevail.* Then let the ordinary methods of influencing public opinion be perseveringly employed. Let the press be enlisted in the work, and carry cogent arguments and stirring appeals to many minds. Let as many as possible of our three thousand periodicals plead the cause of religion and humanity with their readers. Let tracts be scattered on the four winds of heaven, and enforce, by every consideration of duty and interest, this momentous subject. And while the eye is thus reached, let the ear be saluted with the same pleas. Let the sanctuary resound with it, and the eloquence of the forty thousand pulpits of our land be brought to bear upon this theme, which is so worthy of its highest efforts. Let the popular lecturer adopt it for his subject, and the Christian statesman, as one from which he cannot withhold his voice. Let Christians converse upon it with one another, and become each an apostle of peace to his neighbor. Let all pious influences thus be brought to bear upon the work, and no effort spared which can in any way assist it.

Who can doubt as to what would be the inevitable result of such efforts? They would rapidly mould public opinion, open the eyes of the intelligent and candid of our nation to the evils of war and the importance of uninterrupted peace, and few years would elapse before this Christian people would unitedly demand that there be *no more war*. The voice of the nation would utter itself with a force which no ruler would dare resist, and the general sentiment of the people would be made *the law of the land.* Our legislators would not be slow in discovering the proper substitute for war, and whatever course might be pursued by other nations, this one would "not learn war any more." Nor would the effect of these special efforts, put forth by American Christians, end here. This nation would then utter its voice to others, and by means of faithful and repeated efforts, would probably induce them to join with it in determining some plan of arbitration which should for ever stay the flow of human blood; and *what would there then be to prevent the reign of peace on earth?*

These views may appear chimerical to some, but we believe them to be founded in reason and good sense, and justified by both experience and prophecy. They will not, indeed, be realized by means of any slight, partial endeavors. Their fulfilment will require the exercise of our united, prayerful energies; and until these are afforded, we must remain liable at any moment to be plunged into war. But we repeat, let such special efforts as have been described, or even a tithe of them, be made, and if there is any connection between cause and effect, or the means and the end—if there is truth in experience, and certainty in the word of God, the blessings of peace may soon be secured for our nation, and at no distant day made prevalent throughout the globe.

CHAPTER XV.

THE FUTURE TRIUMPH OF PEACE.

THOSE who toil and pray in this noble cause may be animated with the *certainty of success.* Their labors will be no mere doubtful experiment, but the accomplishment of the world's divinely appointed destiny. In addition to all the motives drawn from the past and present, a most sublime one is afforded by the predicted future. The Christian knows that the goal of universal peace is no imaginary one. It stands out distinctly before him, painted by the finger of eternal truth, a blissful, glowing reality. Whatever obstacles may lie in the way, that goal shall be reached. This is as certain as that idolatry shall cease, and the gospel triumph throughout the world. The same word of God which assures us of the one, foretells the other. The same almighty truth and power that are pledged for the one, are pledged for the other.

Indeed, the two are so intimately connected, that we might infer the prevalence of peace from the promised prevalence of gospel truth. It is impossible that the precepts of the Bible should be generally received and obeyed, without causing wars to cease; impossible that the earth should be "full of the knowledge of the Lord," without being full of love and harmony; impossible that "all nations" should "serve him," and yet any so palpably disobey him as to engage in war; and impossible that Jesus should have "dominion from sea to sea," and yet men remain under the dominion of hateful and wicked passions. If "every knee shall bow" to Christ, if the Son shall have the heathen for his inheritance, and the uttermost parts of the earth for his possession, and if "the Lord shall be king over all the earth," then it cannot be doubted for an instant that *peace shall prevail.*

We are not left, however, merely to infer this sublime truth. Among the future blessings to our race foretold by prophecy, this one stands out in bold relief. It is a theme upon which the pen of inspiration loved to linger. The Holy Spirit has invested it with the most attractive imagery, and painted it in glowing hues upon the scroll of this world's destiny. "The wolf also shall dwell with the lamb, and the leopard shall lie down with the kid; and the calf, and the young lion, and the fatling together; and a little child shall lead them. They shall not hurt nor destroy in all my holy mountain; for the earth shall be full of the knowledge of the Lord, as the waters cover the sea." Isaiah 11:6, 9. "And in that day will I make a covenant for them with the beasts of the field, and with the fowls of heaven, and with the creeping things of the ground: and I will break the bow and the sword and the battle out of the earth, and will make them to lie down safely." Hosea 2:18. "He maketh wars to cease unto the end of the earth; he breaketh the bow, and cutteth the spear in sunder; he burneth the chariot in the fire." Psa. 46:9. "And I will cut off the chariot from Ephraim, and the horse from Jerusalem, and the battle-bow shall be cut off: and he shall speak peace unto the heathen: and his dominion shall be from sea even to sea, and from the river even to the ends of the earth." Zech. 9:10. "And the work of righteousness shall be peace; and the effect of righteousness, quietness and assurance for ever. And my people shall dwell in a peaceable habitation, and in sure dwellings, and in quiet resting-places." Isaiah 32:17, 18. "The mountains shall bring peace to the people, and the little hills, by righteousness. In his days shall the righteous flourish; and abundance of peace so long as the moon endureth." Psa. 72:3, 7. "For ye shall go out with joy, and be led forth with peace." Isaiah 55:12. "And it shall come to pass in the last days, that the mountain of the Lord's house shall be established in the top of the mountains, and shall be exalted above the hills; and all nations shall flow unto it. And they shall beat their swords into ploughshares, and their spears into pruning-hooks: nation shall not lift up sword against nation, neither shall they learn war any more." Isaiah 2:2, 4.

What an enchanting prospect is here opened to the eye of Christian faith! Gladly we turn our gaze from scenes of strife and slaughter, to those of love and peace by which they shall be succeeded; and refresh our minds with the contemplation of that bright era when there shall be "*on earth, peace.*" We have beheld the ravages of war, and the view of its terrible havoc has prompted the inquiry, "Shall the sword devour for ever?" We scan the narrow horizon of earth for a reply, but the question comes back upon the aching heart unanswered; and only its echo salutes the ear, mockingly shouting in the din and clangor of "wars and rumors of wars," "*for ever.*" But look up, O world of sufferers, look up to heaven, and if your ears are attuned to its language, you shall hear a "still small voice," yet one that is every day waxing louder and louder, and which in coming years shall speak in all the authoritative thunders of divine omnipotence, saying, "*I will break the bow, and the sword, and the battle out of the earth.*" It is the same voice which once "said, Let there be light; and there was light." It is enough. "Thus saith the Lord," and we need no other assurance that the world is to be thus blessed. "Thus saith the Lord," and his promise, as it comes pealing with such emphasis from the throne of the universe, satisfies every pious heart, and thrills us with the confident expectation of this wished-for period.

The time shall come when all men shall be knit together in one common brotherhood; when no deed of violence shall crimson their hands, and no thought of enmity blacken their hearts; when the air of heaven shall no longer echo with the clash of arms and the curses of men upon their fellows, but shall everywhere resound with the high praises of Christ, "our peace;" when neither the rising nor setting sun shall gleam upon bristling bayonets and clashing swords, but both shall everywhere smile upon bounteous harvests and scenes of peaceful industry; when the Sun of righteousness shall scatter the gross darkness of both Christian and heathen lands, and suffuse every nook and corner of the earth with its pure radiance, and "the work of righteousness shall be *peace;*" when neighbor and neighbor, family and family, nation and nation, man and man shall be animated by one and the same principle, *love;* when every relation of life, great or small, and every phase of human intercourse, limited or extended, shall be made beautiful and holy and happy, because imbued with love; and when, above all, every soul shall be at peace with God, in whom shall centre supremely their united affections. That time shall come, "for the word of the Lord hath spoken it;" and that word assures us, "I the Lord will hasten it in his time." "*Even so, come, Lord Jesus.*"

This promised period of peace is not portrayed in God's word for the mere purpose of happy contemplation, but in order to impel us to faithful efforts towards its realization. We may not satisfy ourselves with simply gazing upon the goal at a distance, and lying quietly upon our oars with folded hands and half-closed eyes, as if some propitious breeze would waft us lazily towards it. It will never be reached until men awake to a sense of their own obligations to labor and pray for its attainment. We should therefore regard these predictions rather as motives to effort, than as excuses for indolence. Let us derive from them new incentives of *hope* and *duty*.

1. As a pledge of success, they should quicken us *to labor hopefully*. Do we *believe* these promises of the sacred word? Do we believe that they are no poetic fictions, but truths of God? Then how great is our encouragement! Whatever be the difficulties attending this work, we descry beyond them all *a perfect success*. Men may deride; the faithless may scoff at the idea of so changing the sentiment of mankind; governments may turn a deaf ear to our entreaties and our reasons; war may once more envelope

the earth with its baleful influences, and the gathering clouds of passion may again seem to blot out this star of hope; but we need not despair. Faith's eye can still discern that star, beaming on brightly as ever, far beyond their reach. Satan may muster all hellish forces against us, and not lightly suffer that curse to be abolished whose victims have so peopled his infernal kingdom; but mightier is He who is for us, than he who is against us. The promise is still ours, and until he can extinguish our faith in God, and obliterate those lines which the finger of God has traced, he cannot destroy our assurance of ultimate success. We may die with the promise unfulfilled; whole generations of Christians may achieve their portion of the work, and transmit it to those who follow them, but there will be no room for despair. The issue of the conflict is certain.

> "Truth, struck to earth, shall rise again:
> The eternal years of God are hers;
> While error, wounded, writhes in pain,
> And dies amid her worshippers."

With our eyes fixed upon the inevitable result, let us press forward in the path which God has marked out. We are accustomed, in toiling for ordinary blessings, to labor earnestly for uncertain good. What zeal ought to mark our efforts in this cause, whose *success is undoubted!* Let every bosom be animated with unwavering hope; and let that hope be, amid the tempestuous ravings of earthly or hellish fury, "as an anchor of the soul, both sure and steadfast."

2. We may derive from these promises a lesson of our *duty.* Is peace and concord to mark the millennium? Then it will be so because they are men's duty; and as duty is the same in every age, those dispositions are equally binding upon us *now.* Whatever will be right in that day, is right in this; and every thing that is now opposed to the spirit which shall then animate mankind, is manifestly wrong. There can hardly be afforded a better illustration of the practical bearings of the gospel upon human intercourse than this fact, that with the future prevalence of its doctrines, peace also shall abound. Instead, then, of conforming our conduct to the standard of the world's past history, which is obviously low and imperfect, let us conform to the lofty one held out before us in its more perfect future. Or rather, let us obey that gospel whose fulfil-

ment will lie at the foundation of every millennial blessing. Let the promises of the word explain and enforce its precepts, and let the church feel that she is best obeying its precepts when she is hastening the fulfilment of its promises.

The Bible is a full and complete revelation of the divine will, and affords us the same rule of right that shall hereafter unite all men in the "bonds of peace." There is to be no new gospel, and the millennium will be nothing more nor less than a general and close conformity to the gospel we now possess. It is only because we do not now obey it as we ought, that we do not now enjoy its blessings. The glaring contrast that exists between the world's present and future happiness, is a contrast between present and future views of, and faithfulness in duty. Can it be questioned which of the two views is correct? The bright era to which the church looks so hopefully forward, is a perpetual rebuke to her present disobedience. The glowing prophetic pictures which we have contemplated will be a standing reproof to the church and the world until they shall be fulfilled, for they express the *standard of human duty.* Then let each individual behold in the anticipated triumph of peace, a view of the spirit and conduct *now* required of him. Let every nation discern in it an imperative obligation *now* to conform to that gospel which shall then so happily regulate all national intercourse. As soon as this is done peace will reign, but not before. As long as men content themselves with merely *looking upon* the beautiful goal, and forget that they must themselves *push forward to it,* that goal will be unattained; and it will be so, not from any backwardness in God, but as the result of human failures in duty.

If these views be correct, is it not a libel upon the church's whole history since the gospel was first given her, that wars have not long ago ceased in Christian nations? Shall we, brethren in Christ, still perpetuate that libel? Shall the sounds of battle, the shrieks of the dying, the wails of perishing souls, and so many other piteous accents of human woe fall on our ears unheeded? Shall the voice of God, addressing us from the throne of his providence, and by the word of his grace—now in tones of stern command, and now in those of sweet encouragement—now by precept, and now by promise—fail to affect us? With the blessing before us, and the gospel which is to secure it in our hands; with heaven's power above us pledged to our assistance; with human sorrows all about us craving to be relieved; and with conscience within us urging to our duty—shall not that duty be fulfilled, the means employed, and the blessing gained? Let us arise in the strength of God, gird ourselves for the work, and with uplifted heads, and eyes upraised to heaven, resolve that *the plague shall be stayed.* Let us become conscious of our dignity and privilege as honored with an embassy of love to men, and let nothing divert us from it. Let us labor to extend the pure leaven of gospel principles throughout the great mass of humanity, "till the whole is leavened." Let the "grain of mustard seed" even now become "a tree," extend its branches to the light and air of heaven, until it overshadows all nations, and celestial messengers of love, like birds, shall "lodge in the branches thereof," and its leaves be "for the healing of the nations." So shall the church, by fulfilling her appointed duty, embrace her promised destiny. So shall one cloud after another be scattered before the rays of the Sun of righteousness, until it shall shine with splendor in a clear sky, and vivify every soul with its light and heat of universal love. "Oh, house of Jacob, *come ye, and let us walk in the light of the Lord.*"

CHAPTER XVI.

CONCLUDING APPEAL.

WE have now exhibited the *Right Way*, or the application of the Gospel to the intercourse of individuals and nations. It only remains that we affectionately appeal to the heart and conscience of every reader of this volume, thus to apply that gospel to himself and others.

I. Let it be your first endeavor to *conform your own heart and life to its dictates.* Consider each of the divine precepts which have met your eye while reading these pages, as possessed of an equal claim to your obedience with every other command of God. View them as matters of *personal* duty and *personal* interest. Turn your gaze within, and explore, by the aid of truth's clear light, the deepest recesses of your soul. Drag out from their lurking places every fiend of passion; then sit in judgment upon them, and condemn and crucify them together with that "old man" sin, whose offspring they are, and whose features they possess. Are they not enemies to your peace; malignant foes to God and your soul; hateful tyrants who silently forge within you the chains of a disgraceful bondage, and seek to enslave your deathless spirit with shameful fetters? Then, in the exercise of a Christlike, godlike spirit, resolve that as far as in you lies, and as far as divine grace shall aid you, you will shake them off, and no longer sin and suffer from them. Transfer your hatred, if you have any, from outward to inward foes. Against them you may be "angry, and sin not."

Would you avoid contention? Then obey from the heart that "royal law," which will forestall it with holy, tender sympathies. Would you convert your enemies into friends? Then cease to befriend your passions, but treat them as your enemies. Would you fulfil duty, and do that which is right towards God and man? Then fulfil the gospel, and exercise love to God and man. Would you be like Jesus? Then imitate him in forgiving and blessing men. Would you be happy? Then foster those kind dispositions and sweet affections whose absence is misery, but whose presence is delight. Would you be glorious? Would you achieve that which is lofty, and ennobling to humanity, and nearly allied to divinity? Then aspire to that glory of the wise man—which is also the glory of God—"to pass over a transgression." Make Christ your pattern, and the gospel your rule of duty. Apply the precepts of Jesus to every relation in life, and let them be, in all your "walk and conversation," as a lamp to your feet and a light to your path.

II. Having done your utmost to mould your own life and character to these precepts, you will feel it to be your duty and privilege to *commend them to others, and lead them into the right way.* Do this by *example.* Let your conduct exert a benign influence upon all who witness it, and attest to every beholder the power and beauty of the spirit of Christ. So exhibit, in all their attractive aspect, the mild graces of love, forgiveness, and long-suffering, that they shall sweetly win upon every heart. To these silent and unobtrusive, yet eloquent pleas for peace, add frequent, prayerful, and well-directed *efforts.* Inculcate it upon the family as the main-spring of its peculiar joys. Let its language be made to old and young "familiar as household words." Teach it to the school, as a lesson never to be unlearned, as an indispensable part of both youthful and manly enjoyment, and as an important preparation for active life. Urge it upon the Sabbath-scholar, and imbue the opening minds of the rising generation with that lovely wisdom, whose "ways are ways of pleasantness, *and all her paths are peace.*" Commend it to the neighbor, as the secret of happy intercourse with those about him. Cultivate it in the church, as an imperative obligation, and an essential part of its piety and prosperity. With a heart alive to its importance, improve every opportunity of pressing its claims, and exerting in its favor all the influence that God has given you. So shall you experience in your own peaceful life, and in the sublime consciousness of duty done and good conferred, a fulfilment of the benediction, "*Blessed are the peacemakers; for they shall be called the children of God.*"

III. By the employment of these and other means, *aim steadfastly at the goal of national peace.* Let your sympathies extend so widely as to embrace the globe, and let your views of duty and faith in God animate you to every effort towards abolishing the curse of *war*. Be not diverted from this aim by the thought that one person can accomplish but little towards securing it. Remember that all great reforms must begin with individuals, and that the masses of the people cannot instantly be persuaded to yield up their deep-rooted prejudices, but that the change must begin with each one separately. We must infuse right principles into the lesser and more limited relations of life; and in proportion as this is done, their application will become gradually extended, until the same views and feelings which govern the family, the neighborhood, and the church, will be found working out their glorious results in the nation and throughout the world. Diffuse, therefore, through all the circle of your influence the leaven of a healthful sentiment; and remember that it is by God's blessing upon the united efforts, and God's answer to the united prayers of many such as you, that war is to be abolished.

Perhaps you cannot influence governments and rulers; but may you not put in motion, or assist the means which shall influence them? Perhaps you cannot bring eloquence to bear upon this theme; but may not your pen become "mightier than the sword" by doing something towards staying its ravages? Or cannot you exert an influence upon other minds, and enlist them in this work? Or cannot you contribute of your substance towards disseminating right principles upon this subject? Who cannot *pray* for so inestimable a blessing? Here is a means that is not denied to any, and one more effective than tongue, or pen, or sword. The prayer of faith can arise above the din of battle and the strife of a world at war with God and with itself, and its answer can say to the discordant elements, "*Peace; be still.*" Whatever else you do or leave undone in this work, "pray for the peace of Jerusalem," and for that of the whole world. O that the cry for peace might go up to God from every pious heart with such effectual fervor, that He who heareth prayer should arise in the might and majesty of his omnipotence, and "speak peace to the heathen!"

1. We appeal to all *rulers and legislators*. God has imposed upon you a solemn responsibility, and you cannot evade it. He has committed to your guardianship the lives and interests of many of his creatures, and you must

account to him for the manner in which you discharge that trust. He has placed in your hands the open Bible, and revealed to you his will, which is the only rule of human right. Will you recklessly trample upon his sovereign edicts, despise his authority, and brave his vengeance? Will you, by encouraging or declaring war, wreck the peace and prosperity, the virtue, the happiness, and the lives of those committed to your charge?

Pause ere you do it, and honestly consider the end of such a course. Look upon the peaceful homes of the nation, and ask whether *yours* shall be the hand to mar and blight them. Look at its prosperous commercial interests, and ask whether your hand shall whelm them in destruction. Look at our thronged sanctuaries, and all the various influences of morality and religion which are the country's safeguard, and ask whether your hand shall overthrow them, and deluge the land with vice and irreligion. Look forward to the judgment-day, and ask whether you shall be willing then to answer for the lives and *souls* of thousands. Oh, listen to the voice of humanity, of patriotism, and of religion, and exert your power for the good of men. Let your voice be heard in the national councils echoing the growing sentiments of Christians and philanthropists, and demanding that war shall be no more. So, whether successful or not, your hands shall be free from blood, and your name transmitted with honor to posterity.

2. We appeal to all *citizens*. Upon you especially devolves this work, for you are in this land the real sovereigns. It is your voices which sway the national councils, and your minds which resolve upon national conduct. You have the power, citizens of America, to stay the plague of war, if you have the will. It is for you to speak the word, and peace shall be made the law of the nation, and secured to yourselves and your posterity. We therefore ask you seriously to contemplate the blessings which may thus be perpetuated, and the curse which may thus be banished — the national glory and prosperity to be thus gained, and the shame and disaster to be thus avoided. Survey your smiling fields—your thriving commerce and manufactures—your schools, colleges, and churches—your homes and firesides: let the view of these impel you to the employment of

those means, and the utterance of that voice, which shall abolish this bane of civil, social, and domestic life. As you love your country, and would secure its real and lasting welfare, let peace, more potent than armies or navies, surround the nation with its perpetual bulwark of defence!

3. We appeal to all *philanthropists.* Has not this moral plague long enough blighted our earth, and withered human joys? Is it not time that heaven's own antidote be applied to it? Oh, then, heed the cries and groans of so many of your fellow-creatures; be moved by the tears of widows and orphans; listen to the appeals of suffering, outraged humanity; and then, your heart full of pitying emotion and your mind resolute with holy purposes, spare no effort to redeem men from this plague!

4. We appeal to the *young.* We turn with peculiar pleasure and strong hope to the rising generation, and would enlist their active labors in this work. Make the principles of the gospel your rule of life, and begin early to practise and commend them. They will prove to you the surest means of success and happiness, and go far towards rendering your path upon earth

that smooth and flowery one which youth always dreams it may be. It is only by fervently loving God and your race, that you can extract from life its choicest sweets. To you we especially look for zealous efforts in behalf of *national peace*, for your minds are comparatively unprejudiced and open to the conviction of its necessity, and your hearts and hands are strong to resolve and act upon that conviction. Let this cause take deep hold upon your inmost sympathies. Youth of America, can you desire a loftier honor, or can you better prove your patriotism, and signalize yourselves as benefactors of mankind and *as Christians*, than by an earnest devotedness to this work? Would that you might be the favored ones to whom it shall be given to introduce the reign of universal peace! Such, there is every reason to believe, you may become if you will; and God will assuredly smile upon your efforts, and make glorious and blessed *the generation of peace-makers.*

5. We appeal to *women.* If any are interested in this cause, you are; for upon you have fallen many of the chief evils of war. Then exert wisely your influence in favor of peace.

If you would not have your homes made desolate, and your hearts torn with keenest pangs; if you would not have earth's fondest ties cruelly rent asunder, and your lives clouded with heaviest griefs—enlist in this work something of that zeal and enthusiasm which characterize so many of your benevolent enterprises. By example, by persuasion, by entreaty, seek to influence the minds about you in its favor. Urge it upon fathers, husbands, sons, and brothers. Mould the infant minds intrusted to you with a hatred of every form of strife. Carefully banish from their youthful sports the toys and pictures of war; and among their earliest and most indelible impressions, let there be, not that admiration of martial dress and exploits which so often poisons their minds, but a deep, unalterable abhorrence of every thing pertaining to this horrid crime. This is a cause which well becomes you. It sits most gracefully upon the female character, affording that loveliest of ornaments, which, we are told, "is in the sight of God of great price," "even the ornament of a meek and quiet spirit."

6. We appeal to all *ministers of the gospel.* Upon you devolves the duty and the glorious

privilege of bearing God's messages to human hearts. "Embassadors for Christ," your embassy is one of *peace*. The very terms of your commission imply it; for how can you faithfully "preach the gospel," without publishing abroad those great duties which, as has been shown, the gospel so strongly inculcates? It is a safe rule to guide the preacher in the selection of his themes, and in judging of the prominence to be given to particular subjects, to notice the frequency and extent to which they are insisted upon in the Bible. The word is a complete system, and gives to each truth its proper eminence and comparative importance. It is arranged with such symmetry, that it is as perfect as a whole as it is in each separate part. They who would reproduce the edifice in others, must observe the same harmony of proportions; and not only "declare the whole counsel of God," but assign to each portion of it that prominence which God has given it.

If this view be correct, has not one great feature of the religion of Christ been kept much in the background? The precepts relating to human intercourse were deemed by our Lord of sufficient importance to claim frequent and earnest reiteration. They are no less so at this day, and should be often studied and enforced by the gospel preacher. Had the time that has been spent in pulpit discussions of far less moment, and in frivolous and sometimes bitter controversies, been devoted to the preaching of the duties under consideration, not only would much dissension and ill-feeling have been avoided, but there would probably have been no need, at this late day, of efforts to abolish war, for it would have ceased.

Oh, then, watchmen of Zion, "hear the word at the mouth of the Lord," and sound the gospel trumpet in the ears of men. Now, in the soft music of persuasive invitation, let it breathe forth the law of love. Now, in appalling thunders, let it denounce all "bitterness, wrath, and envying." Proclaim from your thousands of pulpits the blessedness of the meek, the merciful, and the peacemakers. It is a fit theme for sacred eloquence, and may well inspire its loftiest efforts. As you exhort to peace with God, commend peace with one another. Exhibit, in their place, these beautiful requirements of Christianity; and let them commend to many souls the religion that teaches them, and lead the church and the world better to estimate and practise them. So shall the song be echoed by many hearts, led by you into paths of peace, "How beautiful upon the mountains are the feet of him that bringeth good tidings—that *publisheth peace.*"

7. We appeal to *all Christians.* Do you believe that the precepts which form the basis of this work are the precepts of Christ? Then we need urge no other plea to remind you of your duty. Will you not obey that voice of Jesus which has addressed you? Let the sounds of contention in which it has been almost drowned for centuries, only add to its emphasis, and clothe it with redoubled thunders of command, and yet more pleading accents of entreaty. Embrace with joy and gratitude the law of love, and let your inmost soul become imbued with its sweet influences. Then seek to apply it to the community, the church, the nation, and the world. Put forth your hand to the work of abolishing war. In proportion as you labor and pray for that consummation, you will obey an important part of the gospel, foster religion and morality, and hasten the millennial glory. Wield diligently those

forces which God has placed at your command, and which only Christians can adequately employ. *Labor* with untiring diligence. "*Pray* without ceasing." Pour into the ears of God and man your pleas and your entreaties. Hear the mingled groans of the wounded and dying, and the sighs of the widow and the fatherless, and let them quicken you to effort. See the countless and gigantic iniquities of this accursed system. Think of the eternal writhings of the souls whom it destroys. Hear, added to voices that plead from earth and wail from hell, the tones of Jehovah's plain commands. Let them awaken every energy to the task of an unquestioning obedience. See that bow of promise which spans the centuries of darkness, and assures you that the deluge of human blood shall one day cease to flow, and the nations "not learn war any more." Let it incite you to hope and duty.

As you would be happy; as you would promote the sum of human bliss, and prevent much human woe; as you would remove a mighty stumbling-block from the path of religious progress, and "prepare the way of the Lord" for his peaceful kingdom—O, Christian, cease not to toil and pray in this work! All heaven calls out to you—earth pleads—hell warns! The interests of humanity, truth, justice, and religion—the hopes of those that are ready to perish—all that is dear to pious souls—all that is lovely and glowing in the world's future destiny—plead with you, Christian, to engage earnestly in this work!

Let the pleas of duty and interest, of God and man, be heeded. Let the church exert her power, and, by the blessing of God, wipe away this reproach and this guilt from the face of Christendom. So shall that angels' song, which was sung at the birth of Jesus, after having been drowned for centuries in the harsh clamors of human strife, be again heard and echoed by every heart: "*Glory to God in the highest; on earth* PEACE, *good-will towards men.*"

The American Tract Society

PUBLISH A LARGE SELECTION

OF

THE MOST CHOICE PRACTICAL WORKS

IN THE

ENGLISH LANGUAGE;

EMBODIED IN THE

RELIGIOUS (OR PASTOR'S) LIBRARY,
25 Vols. $10.

EVANGELICAL FAMILY LIBRARY,

15 Vols. $5 50.

And the continuation comprising 21 Vols. $7 50.

BESIDES

MORE THAN ONE THOUSAND

Books and Tracts for Old and Young,

MANY OF THEM

BEAUTIFULLY ILLUSTRATED.

www.ingramcontent.com/pod-product-compliance
Lightning Source LLC
LaVergne TN
LVHW020244110826
845151LV00003B/1023

* 9 7 8 1 4 2 5 5 2 8 6 7 6 *